Drawn&Quarterly Showcase
Book One

Publisher, series editor, design, production: Chris Oliveros.

Drawn & Quarterly
Post Office Box 48056
Montreal, Quebec
Canada H2V 4S8
www.drawnandquarterly.com

Printed in Hong Kong in July 2003.

10 9 8 7 6 5 4 3 2 1
National Library of Canada Cataloguing in Publication
Drawn & Quarterly Showcase : one / Kevin Huizenga, Nicolas Robel.
Illustrated short stories.
ISBN 1-896597-62-9
1. Comic books, strips, etc. I. Huizenga, Kevin, 1977— II. Robel, Nicolas, 1974— III. Title.
PN6720.D73 2003   741.5'9   C2003-902732-5

The publisher gratefully acknowledges the support of The Canada Council for The Arts
for its financial support of this edition.

Distributed in the USA and abroad by:
Chronicle Books
85 Second Street
San Francisco, CA 94105
800.722.6657

Distributed in Canada by:
Raincoast Books
9050 Shaughnessy Street
Vancouver, BC V6P 6E5
800.663.5714

An anthology of new illustrated fiction.

Front cover, endpapers:
Nicolas Robel

Pages 7 to 48:
Kevin Huizenga

Pages 51 to 96:
Nicolas Robel

Back cover:
Kevin Huizenga

Kevin Huizenga

Kevin Huizenga was born in 1977 near Chicago and grew up in South Holland, Illinois.

Huizenga has spent the last several years publishing his work in the form of mini-comics. He's written, drawn, photocopied, and stapled about 25 editions to date. For his efforts THE COMICS JOURNAL named him the "Minimalism" Cartoonist of the year in 2001, and he was nominated for two IGNATZ AWARDS for Most Promising New Talent and Outstanding Mini-comic in 2002.

Of his work, Huizenga writes, "My comics are mostly about the suburbs and the midwest, and so far I've tried drawing in a lot of different styles. I've illustrated letters from my Grandma, prayers, Taoist parables, newspaper articles, and drawn a comic based on Chinese landscape painting. Most of my stories are autobiographical, though my last few stories have been mostly fictional."

He now lives and works in St. Louis.

GLENN GANGES

GOOD GRIEF

JUNK,

JUNK,

BILL,

JUNK,

JUNK,

"MAYBE A WINNER"

JUNK,

ULP.

YEP

HERE IT IS

HAVE YOU SEEN

Name: Derrick Marte
DOB: 5/22/1991
Ht.: 4'7" (at age 8)
Wt.: 76 lbs. (at age 8)

EVERY WEEK, USUALLY ON WEDNESDAYS, IN THE STANDARD ASSORTMENT OF JUNK MAIL ADS, SOLICITATIONS, AND CATALOGS THAT JAM UP THE MAILBOX EVERY DAY, THERE IS ONE OF THESE:

SHOP$MART™

HAVE YOU SEEN US™?

NAME:
DOB:
Ht. Wt.
Hair Eyes
Sex Date Miss
From

Last Seen with
DOB
Ht. Wt.
Hair Eyes
Sex
From

RESIDENT AP 2W WSSXXC023
5431 REEJE AVE
GRAND RAPIDS MI   49546

CALL 1-800-THE-LOST

115 children have been safely recovered

USUALLY THERE ARE TWO PICTURES — ONE OF A KID...

Name: Marc Copeland
DOB: 2/20/1992

Last
DOB

AND ONE OF THE PERSON THE KID WAS LAST SEEN WITH. A LOT OF THE TIME THEY HAVE THE SAME LAST NAME.

Last Seen With: Sean Copeland
DOB: 8/8/1968

EVERY WEEK IT'S A MYSTERY — WHAT HAPPENED? WHAT'S THE STORY?

Name: Briana Coates
DOB: 7/19/90
Ht: 3'8" (at age 5)
Wt: 40lbs. (at age 5)
Hair: Lt Brown Eyes: Green
Date Missing: 5/14/96
From: Houston, TX

Last Seen With: Gloria Joy Coates
DOB: 7/3/57
Ht: 5'2" Wt: 100lbs.
Hair: Lt. Brown Eyes: Green
Date Missing: 5/14/96
From: Houston, TX

FATHER? MOTHER? UNCLE? FRIEND? AU PAIR? HOW DO TWO PEOPLE DISAPPEAR? WHY CAN'T ANYONE FIND THEM?

Name: Sheena Vasquez
DOB 2/13/1994
Ht: 4'2" Wt: 45lbs.
Hair: Black Eyes: Black
Date Missing: 1/17/2002
From: Lancaster, PA

Last Seen With: Julianna Dorsett
DOB: 7/9/1974
Ht: 5'1" Wt: 120lbs.
Hair: Black Eyes: Black
Date Missing: 1/17/2002
From: Lancaster, PA

ARE THEY ALL THAT TRICKY? IS AMERICA STILL THAT BIG? MAYBE THEY ARE SAFER LOST?

Name: Pedro Morales-Howat
DOB: 3/4/99
Ht: 2'8" (at 19 mos.)
Wt: 32 lbs. (at 19 mos.)
Hair: Brown Eyes: Brown
Date Missing: 10/17/00
From: Portola, CA

Last Seen With: Kelli Padilla
DOB: 2/1/1978
Ht: 5'6" Wt: 180lbs.
Hair: Blonde Eyes: Hazel
Date Missing: 10/17/00
From: Portola, CA

EVERY WEEK TWO NEW FACES AND YOU IMAGINE THE SCENES IN-BETWEEN.

...ales-Howat
19 mos.)
t 19 mos.)
Eyes: Brown
10/17/00
A, CA

Last Seen...
DOB: 2/1...
Ht: 5'6"...
Hair: Blo...
Date Mis...
From: Po...

YOU'RE LEFT TO IMAGINE SETTINGS USING ONLY LINES LIKE "FROM: SHELBY, NC"

OR "FROM: ANGLETON, TX"

OR "FROM: JASPER, TN"

AND "DATE MISSING: 5/14/1993"

WHERE WE GOING?

DON'T WORRY

JUST GET IN THE CAR, OK HONEY?

DOB: 12/17/87

Hair: Lt Brown

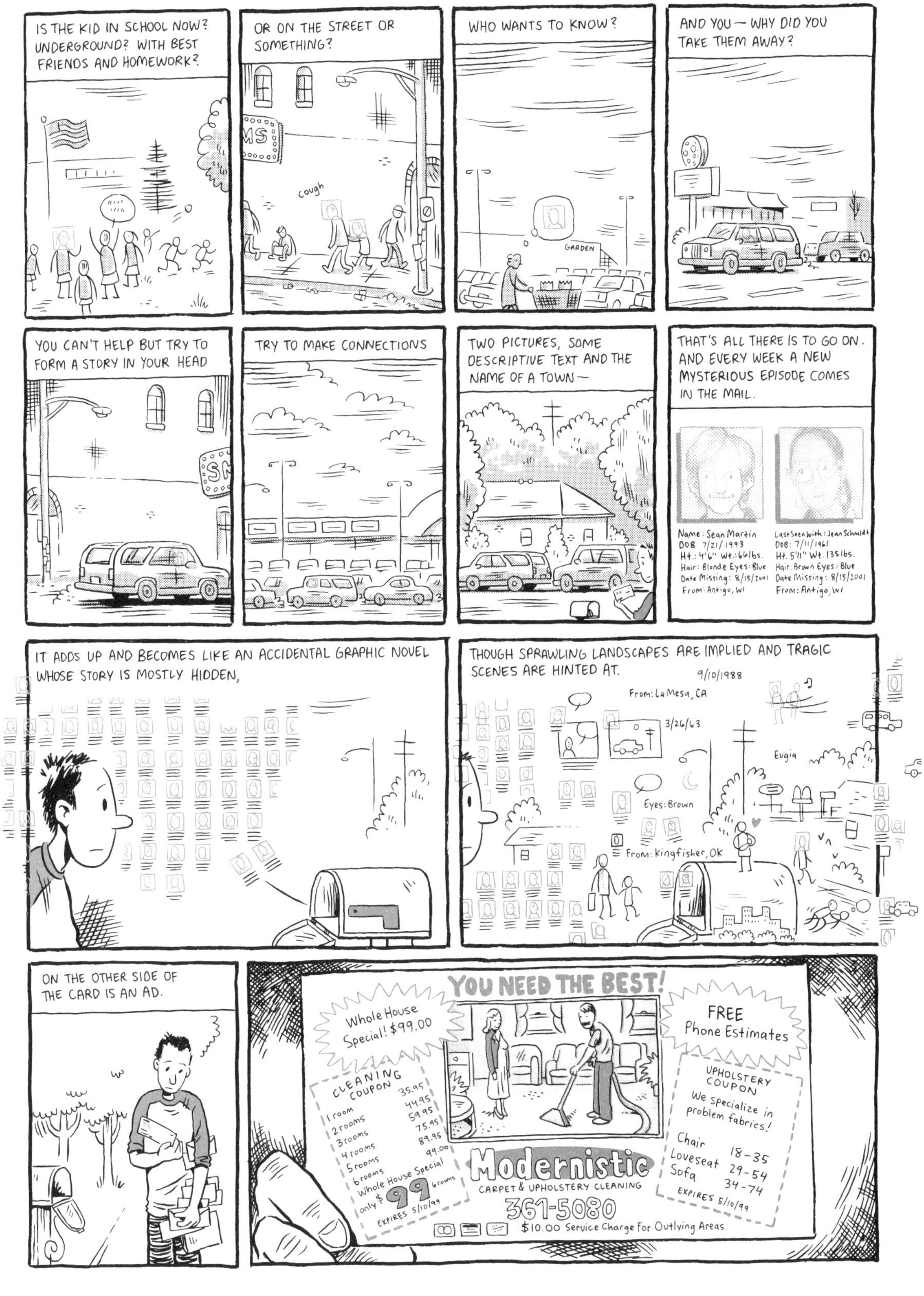

IS THE KID IN SCHOOL NOW? UNDERGROUND? WITH BEST FRIENDS AND HOMEWORK?
OR ON THE STREET OR SOMETHING?
cough
WHO WANTS TO KNOW?
GARDEN
AND YOU — WHY DID YOU TAKE THEM AWAY?
YOU CAN'T HELP BUT TRY TO FORM A STORY IN YOUR HEAD
TRY TO MAKE CONNECTIONS
TWO PICTURES, SOME DESCRIPTIVE TEXT AND THE NAME OF A TOWN —
THAT'S ALL THERE IS TO GO ON. AND EVERY WEEK A NEW MYSTERIOUS EPISODE COMES IN THE MAIL.
Name: Sean Martin
DOB 7/21/1993
Ht.: 4'6" Wt.: 66 lbs.
Hair: Blonde Eyes: Blue
Date Missing: 8/15/2001
From: Antigo, WI
Last Seen With: Jean Schmidt
DOB: 7/11/1961
Ht. 5'11" Wt. 135 lbs.
Hair: Brown Eyes: Blue
Date Missing: 8/15/2001
From: Antigo, WI
IT ADDS UP AND BECOMES LIKE AN ACCIDENTAL GRAPHIC NOVEL WHOSE STORY IS MOSTLY HIDDEN,
THOUGH SPRAWLING LANDSCAPES ARE IMPLIED AND TRAGIC SCENES ARE HINTED AT.
9/10/1988
From: La Mesa, CA
3/26/63
Eugia
Eyes: Brown
From: Kingfisher, OK
ON THE OTHER SIDE OF THE CARD IS AN AD.
YOU NEED THE BEST!
Whole House Special! $99.00
FREE Phone Estimates
CLEANING COUPON
1 room 35.95
2 rooms 44.95
3 rooms 59.95
4 rooms 75.95
5 rooms 89.95
6 rooms 99.00
Whole House Special only $99 6 rooms
EXPIRES 5/10/99
UPHOLSTERY COUPON
We specialize in problem fabrics!
Chair 18–35
Loveseat 29–54
Sofa 34–74
EXPIRES 5/10/99
Modernistic
CARPET & UPHOLSTERY CLEANING
361-5080
$10.00 Service Charge For Outlying Areas

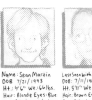

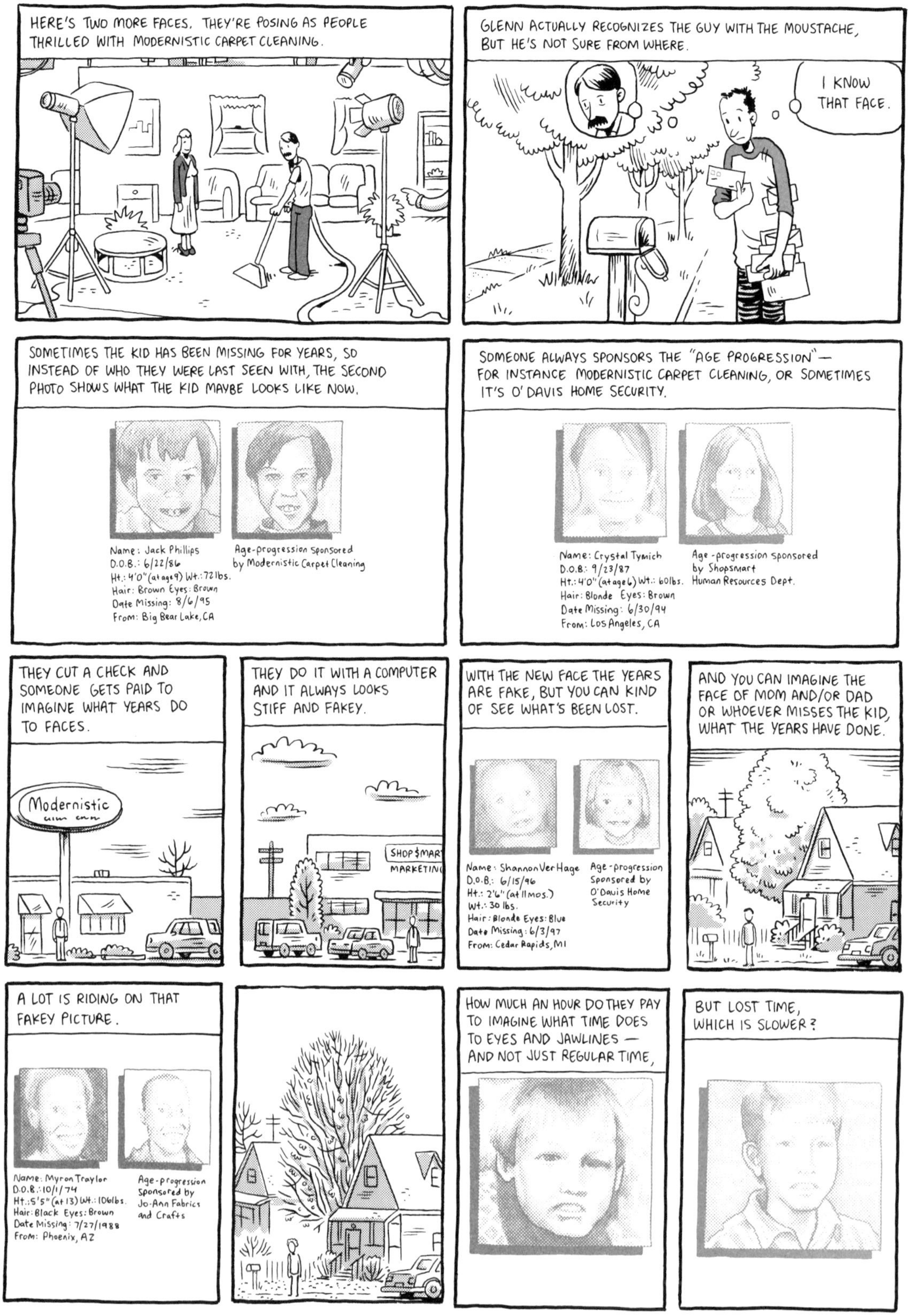

HERE'S TWO MORE FACES. THEY'RE POSING AS PEOPLE THRILLED WITH MODERNISTIC CARPET CLEANING.
GLENN ACTUALLY RECOGNIZES THE GUY WITH THE MOUSTACHE, BUT HE'S NOT SURE FROM WHERE.
I KNOW THAT FACE.
SOMETIMES THE KID HAS BEEN MISSING FOR YEARS, SO INSTEAD OF WHO THEY WERE LAST SEEN WITH, THE SECOND PHOTO SHOWS WHAT THE KID MAYBE LOOKS LIKE NOW.
Name: Jack Phillips
D.O.B.: 6/22/86
Ht.: 4'0" (at age 9) Wt.: 72 lbs.
Hair: Brown Eyes: Brown
Date Missing: 8/6/95
From: Big Bear Lake, CA
Age-progression sponsored by Modernistic Carpet Cleaning
SOMEONE ALWAYS SPONSORS THE "AGE PROGRESSION"— FOR INSTANCE MODERNISTIC CARPET CLEANING, OR SOMETIMES IT'S O'DAVIS HOME SECURITY.
Name: Crystal Tymich
D.O.B: 9/23/87
Ht.: 4'0" (at age 6) Wt.: 60 lbs.
Hair: Blonde Eyes: Brown
Date Missing: 6/30/94
From: Los Angeles, CA
Age-progression sponsored by Shopsmart Human Resources Dept.
THEY CUT A CHECK AND SOMEONE GETS PAID TO IMAGINE WHAT YEARS DO TO FACES.
Modernistic
THEY DO IT WITH A COMPUTER AND IT ALWAYS LOOKS STIFF AND FAKEY.
SHOP$MAR
MARKETIN
WITH THE NEW FACE THE YEARS ARE FAKE, BUT YOU CAN KIND OF SEE WHAT'S BEEN LOST.
Name: Shannon VerHage
D.O.B.: 6/15/96
Ht.: 2'6" (at 11 mos.)
Wt.: 30 lbs.
Hair: Blonde Eyes: Blue
Date Missing: 6/3/97
From: Cedar Rapids, MI
Age-progression Sponsored by O'Davis Home Security
AND YOU CAN IMAGINE THE FACE OF MOM AND/OR DAD OR WHOEVER MISSES THE KID, WHAT THE YEARS HAVE DONE.
A LOT IS RIDING ON THAT FAKEY PICTURE.
Name: Myron Traylor
D.O.B.: 10/1/74
Ht.: 5'5" (at 13) Wt.: 106 lbs.
Hair: Black Eyes: Brown
Date Missing: 7/27/1988
From: Phoenix, AZ
Age-progression Sponsored by Jo-Ann Fabrics and Crafts
HOW MUCH AN HOUR DO THEY PAY TO IMAGINE WHAT TIME DOES TO EYES AND JAWLINES — AND NOT JUST REGULAR TIME,
BUT LOST TIME, WHICH IS SLOWER?

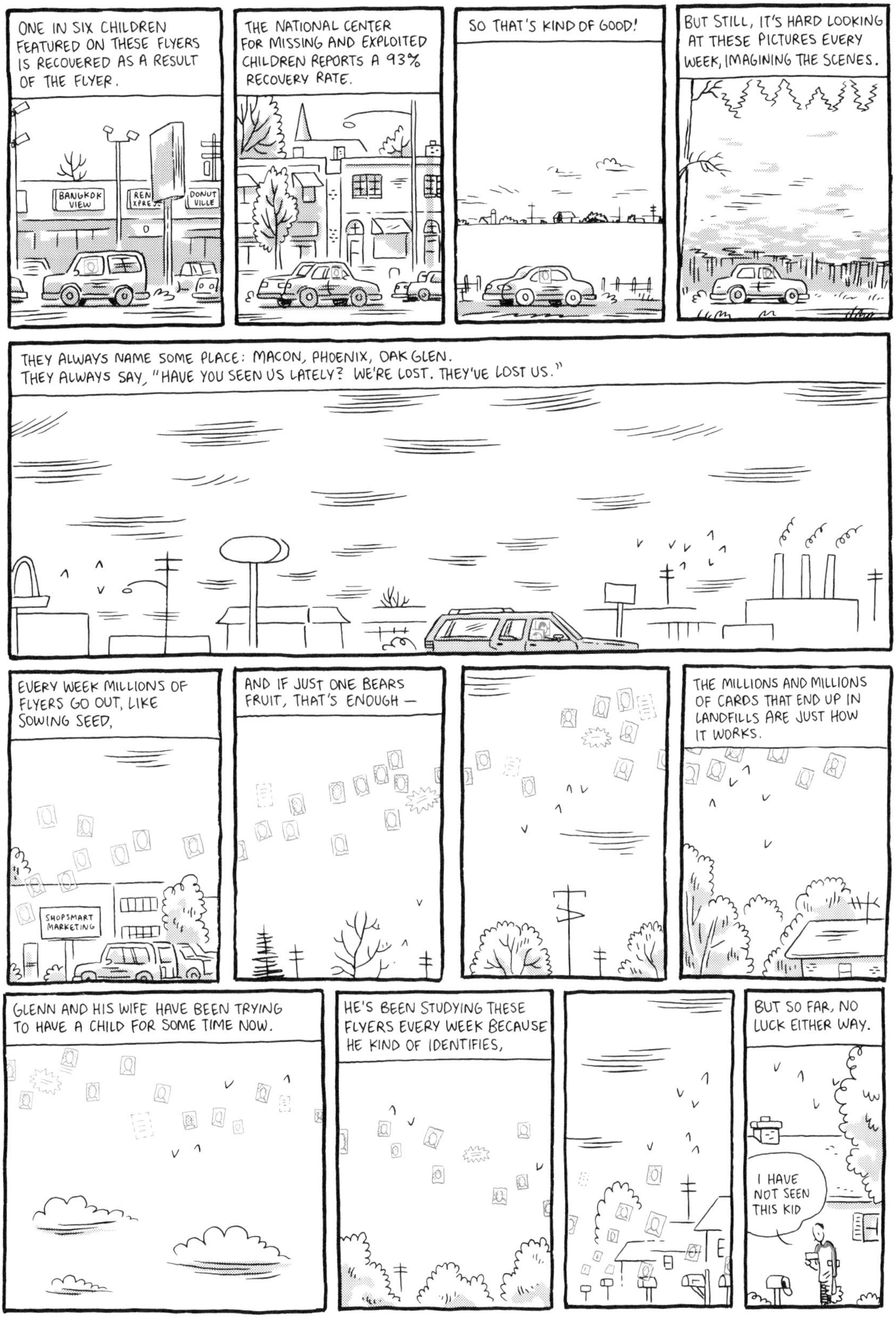

ONE IN SIX CHILDREN FEATURED ON THESE FLYERS IS RECOVERED AS A RESULT OF THE FLYER.
BANGKOK VIEW
DONUT VILLE
THE NATIONAL CENTER FOR MISSING AND EXPLOITED CHILDREN REPORTS A 93% RECOVERY RATE.
SO THAT'S KIND OF GOOD!
BUT STILL, IT'S HARD LOOKING AT THESE PICTURES EVERY WEEK, IMAGINING THE SCENES.
THEY ALWAYS NAME SOME PLACE: MACON, PHOENIX, OAK GLEN.
THEY ALWAYS SAY, "HAVE YOU SEEN US LATELY? WE'RE LOST. THEY'VE LOST US."
EVERY WEEK MILLIONS OF FLYERS GO OUT, LIKE SOWING SEED,
SHOPSMART MARKETING
AND IF JUST ONE BEARS FRUIT, THAT'S ENOUGH —
THE MILLIONS AND MILLIONS OF CARDS THAT END UP IN LANDFILLS ARE JUST HOW IT WORKS.
GLENN AND HIS WIFE HAVE BEEN TRYING TO HAVE A CHILD FOR SOME TIME NOW.
HE'S BEEN STUDYING THESE FLYERS EVERY WEEK BECAUSE HE KIND OF IDENTIFIES,
BUT SO FAR, NO LUCK EITHER WAY.
I HAVE NOT SEEN THIS KID

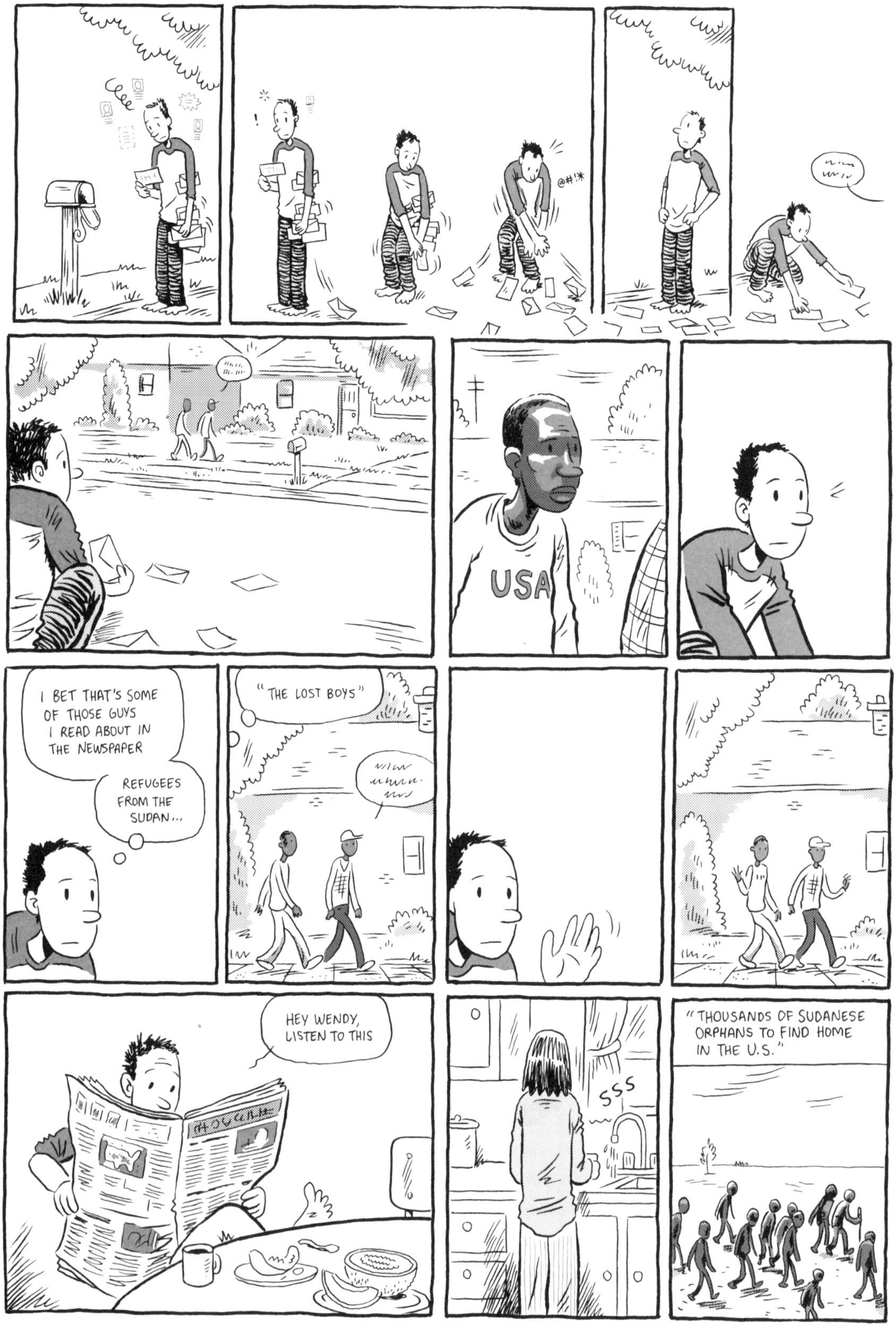
@#!*
I BET THAT'S SOME OF THOSE GUYS I READ ABOUT IN THE NEWSPAPER
REFUGEES FROM THE SUDAN...
"THE LOST BOYS"
HEY WENDY, LISTEN TO THIS
SSS
"THOUSANDS OF SUDANESE ORPHANS TO FIND HOME IN THE U.S."

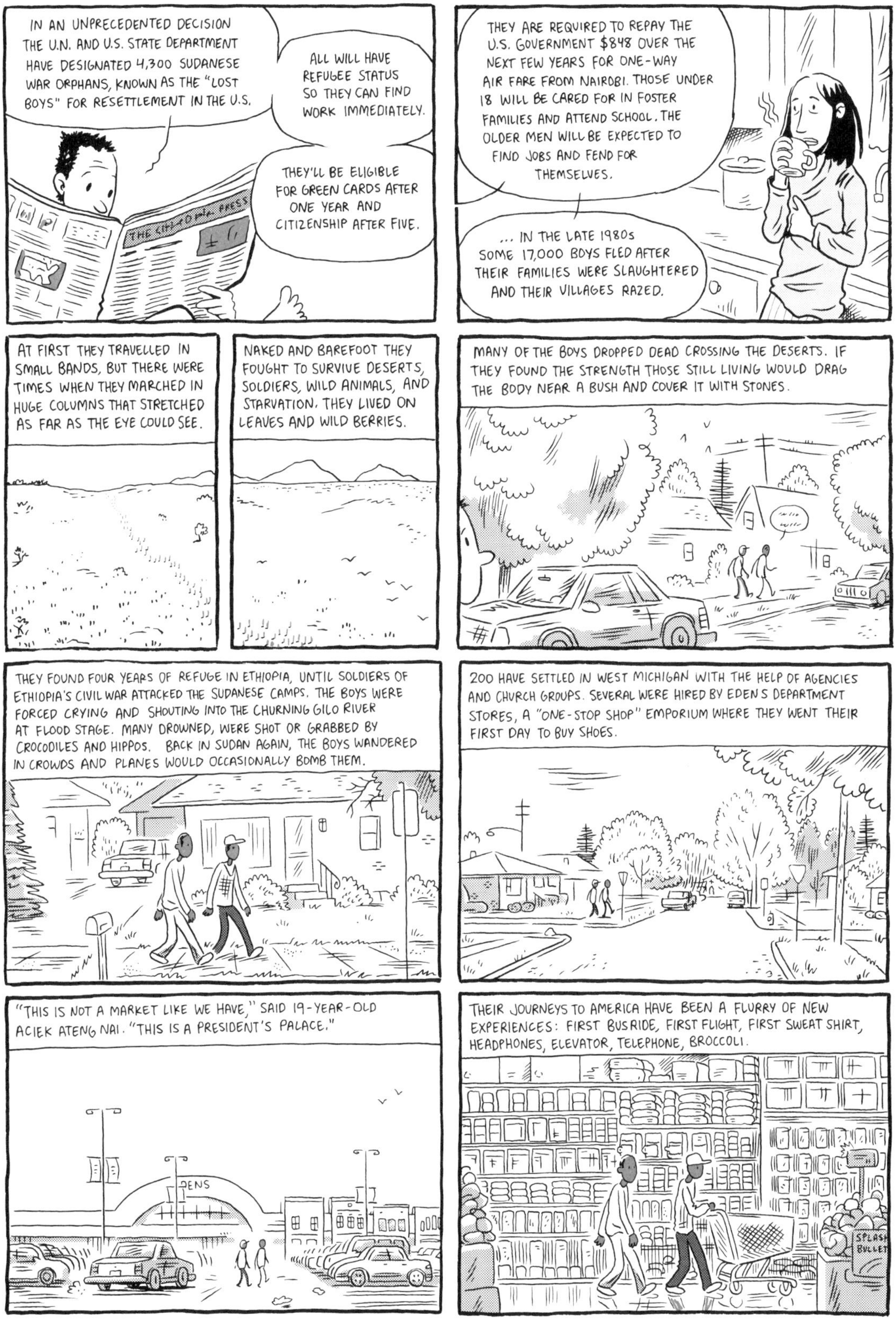
IN AN UNPRECEDENTED DECISION THE U.N. AND U.S. STATE DEPARTMENT HAVE DESIGNATED 4,300 SUDANESE WAR ORPHANS, KNOWN AS THE "LOST BOYS" FOR RESETTLEMENT IN THE U.S.
ALL WILL HAVE REFUGEE STATUS SO THEY CAN FIND WORK IMMEDIATELY.
THEY'LL BE ELIGIBLE FOR GREEN CARDS AFTER ONE YEAR AND CITIZENSHIP AFTER FIVE.
THEY ARE REQUIRED TO REPAY THE U.S. GOVERNMENT $848 OVER THE NEXT FEW YEARS FOR ONE-WAY AIR FARE FROM NAIROBI. THOSE UNDER 18 WILL BE CARED FOR IN FOSTER FAMILIES AND ATTEND SCHOOL. THE OLDER MEN WILL BE EXPECTED TO FIND JOBS AND FEND FOR THEMSELVES.
... IN THE LATE 1980s SOME 17,000 BOYS FLED AFTER THEIR FAMILIES WERE SLAUGHTERED AND THEIR VILLAGES RAZED.
AT FIRST THEY TRAVELLED IN SMALL BANDS, BUT THERE WERE TIMES WHEN THEY MARCHED IN HUGE COLUMNS THAT STRETCHED AS FAR AS THE EYE COULD SEE.
NAKED AND BAREFOOT THEY FOUGHT TO SURVIVE DESERTS, SOLDIERS, WILD ANIMALS, AND STARVATION. THEY LIVED ON LEAVES AND WILD BERRIES.
MANY OF THE BOYS DROPPED DEAD CROSSING THE DESERTS. IF THEY FOUND THE STRENGTH THOSE STILL LIVING WOULD DRAG THE BODY NEAR A BUSH AND COVER IT WITH STONES.
THEY FOUND FOUR YEARS OF REFUGE IN ETHIOPIA, UNTIL SOLDIERS OF ETHIOPIA'S CIVIL WAR ATTACKED THE SUDANESE CAMPS. THE BOYS WERE FORCED CRYING AND SHOUTING INTO THE CHURNING GILO RIVER AT FLOOD STAGE. MANY DROWNED, WERE SHOT OR GRABBED BY CROCODILES AND HIPPOS. BACK IN SUDAN AGAIN, THE BOYS WANDERED IN CROWDS AND PLANES WOULD OCCASIONALLY BOMB THEM.
200 HAVE SETTLED IN WEST MICHIGAN WITH THE HELP OF AGENCIES AND CHURCH GROUPS. SEVERAL WERE HIRED BY EDEN'S DEPARTMENT STORES, A "ONE-STOP SHOP" EMPORIUM WHERE THEY WENT THEIR FIRST DAY TO BUY SHOES.
"THIS IS NOT A MARKET LIKE WE HAVE," SAID 19-YEAR-OLD ACIEK ATENG NAI. "THIS IS A PRESIDENT'S PALACE."
EDENS
THEIR JOURNEYS TO AMERICA HAVE BEEN A FLURRY OF NEW EXPERIENCES: FIRST BUSRIDE, FIRST FLIGHT, FIRST SWEAT SHIRT, HEADPHONES, ELEVATOR, TELEPHONE, BROCCOLI.
SPLASH BULLET

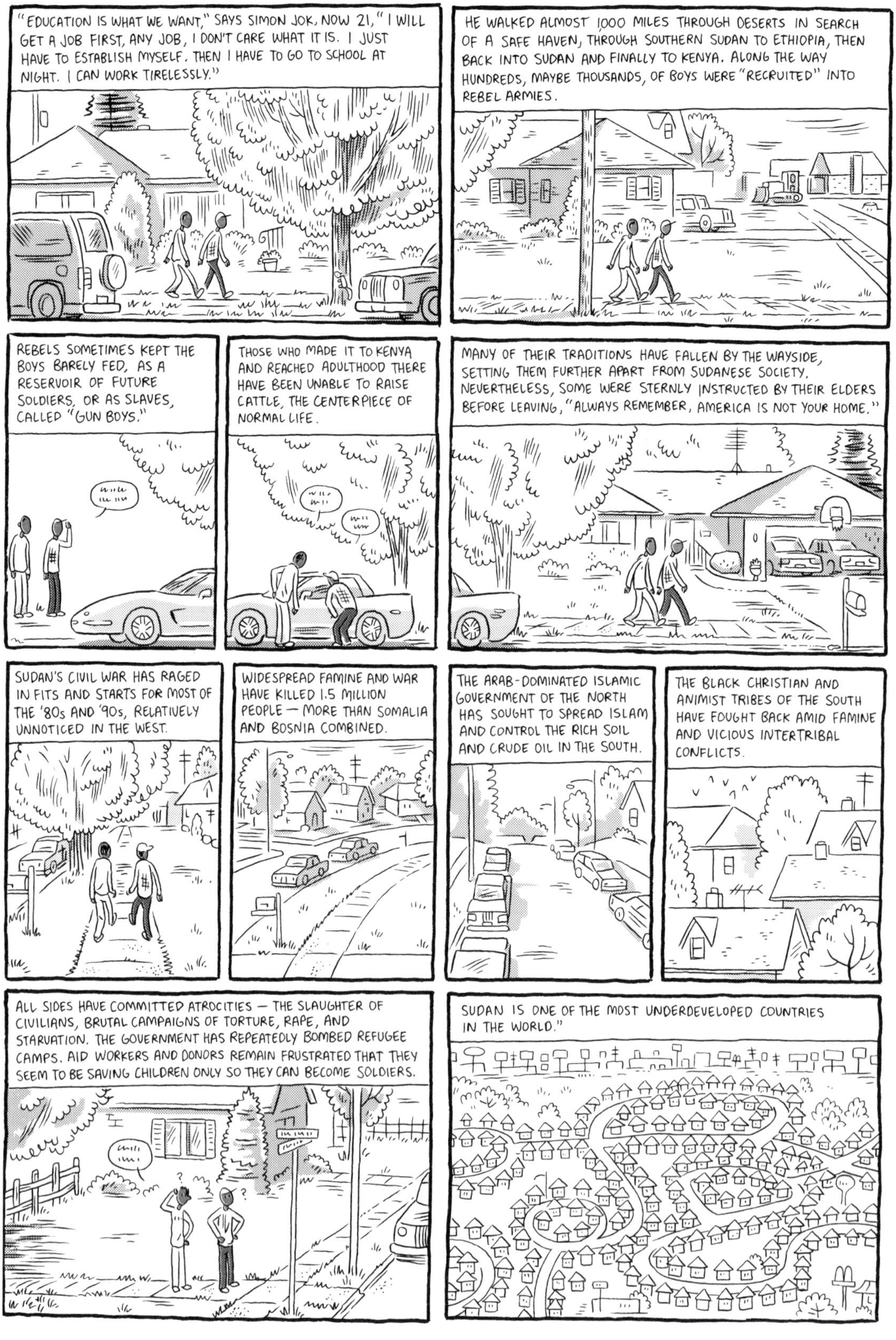
"EDUCATION IS WHAT WE WANT," SAYS SIMON JOK, NOW 21, "I WILL GET A JOB FIRST, ANY JOB, I DON'T CARE WHAT IT IS. I JUST HAVE TO ESTABLISH MYSELF. THEN I HAVE TO GO TO SCHOOL AT NIGHT. I CAN WORK TIRELESSLY."
HE WALKED ALMOST 1,000 MILES THROUGH DESERTS IN SEARCH OF A SAFE HAVEN, THROUGH SOUTHERN SUDAN TO ETHIOPIA, THEN BACK INTO SUDAN AND FINALLY TO KENYA. ALONG THE WAY HUNDREDS, MAYBE THOUSANDS, OF BOYS WERE "RECRUITED" INTO REBEL ARMIES.
REBELS SOMETIMES KEPT THE BOYS BARELY FED, AS A RESERVOIR OF FUTURE SOLDIERS, OR AS SLAVES, CALLED "GUN BOYS."
THOSE WHO MADE IT TO KENYA AND REACHED ADULTHOOD THERE HAVE BEEN UNABLE TO RAISE CATTLE, THE CENTERPIECE OF NORMAL LIFE.
MANY OF THEIR TRADITIONS HAVE FALLEN BY THE WAYSIDE, SETTING THEM FURTHER APART FROM SUDANESE SOCIETY. NEVERTHELESS, SOME WERE STERNLY INSTRUCTED BY THEIR ELDERS BEFORE LEAVING, "ALWAYS REMEMBER, AMERICA IS NOT YOUR HOME."
SUDAN'S CIVIL WAR HAS RAGED IN FITS AND STARTS FOR MOST OF THE '80s AND '90s, RELATIVELY UNNOTICED IN THE WEST.
WIDESPREAD FAMINE AND WAR HAVE KILLED 1.5 MILLION PEOPLE — MORE THAN SOMALIA AND BOSNIA COMBINED.
THE ARAB-DOMINATED ISLAMIC GOVERNMENT OF THE NORTH HAS SOUGHT TO SPREAD ISLAM AND CONTROL THE RICH SOIL AND CRUDE OIL IN THE SOUTH.
THE BLACK CHRISTIAN AND ANIMIST TRIBES OF THE SOUTH HAVE FOUGHT BACK AMID FAMINE AND VICIOUS INTERTRIBAL CONFLICTS.
ALL SIDES HAVE COMMITTED ATROCITIES — THE SLAUGHTER OF CIVILIANS, BRUTAL CAMPAIGNS OF TORTURE, RAPE, AND STARVATION. THE GOVERNMENT HAS REPEATEDLY BOMBED REFUGEE CAMPS. AID WORKERS AND DONORS REMAIN FRUSTRATED THAT THEY SEEM TO BE SAVING CHILDREN ONLY SO THEY CAN BECOME SOLDIERS.
SUDAN IS ONE OF THE MOST UNDERDEVELOPED COUNTRIES IN THE WORLD."

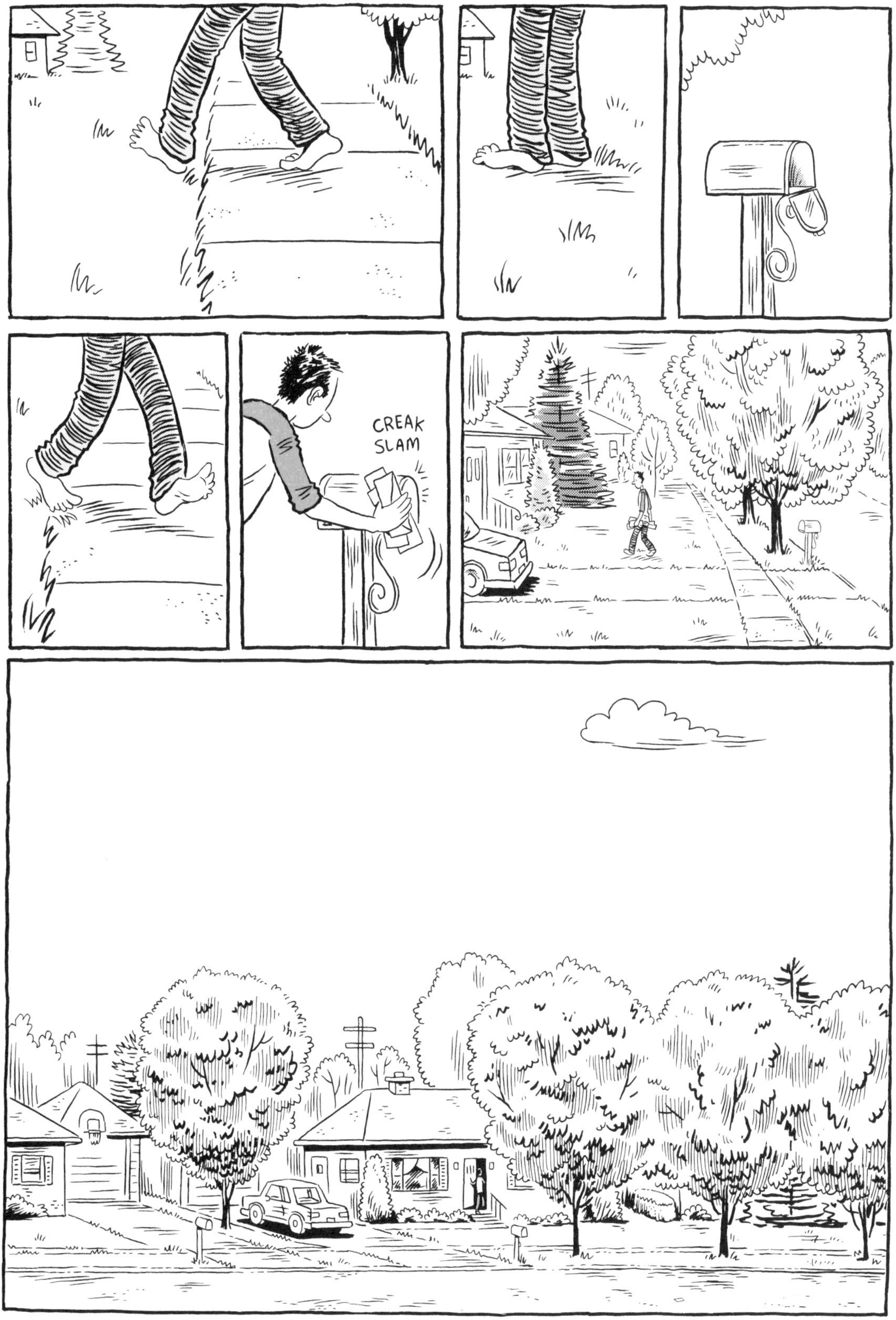
CREAK
SLAM

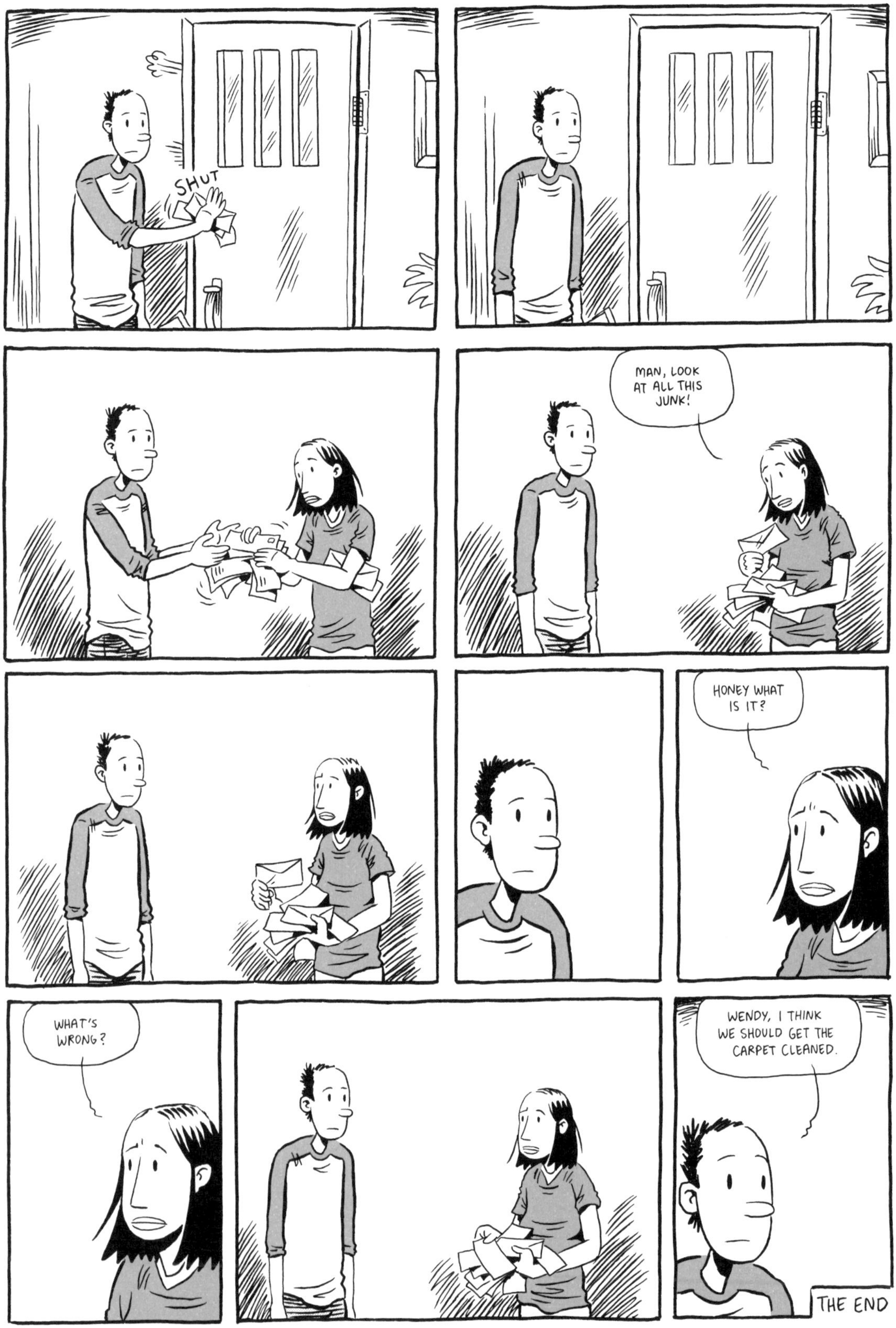
SHUT
MAN, LOOK AT ALL THIS JUNK!
HONEY WHAT IS IT?
WHAT'S WRONG?
WENDY, I THINK WE SHOULD GET THE CARPET CLEANED.
THE END

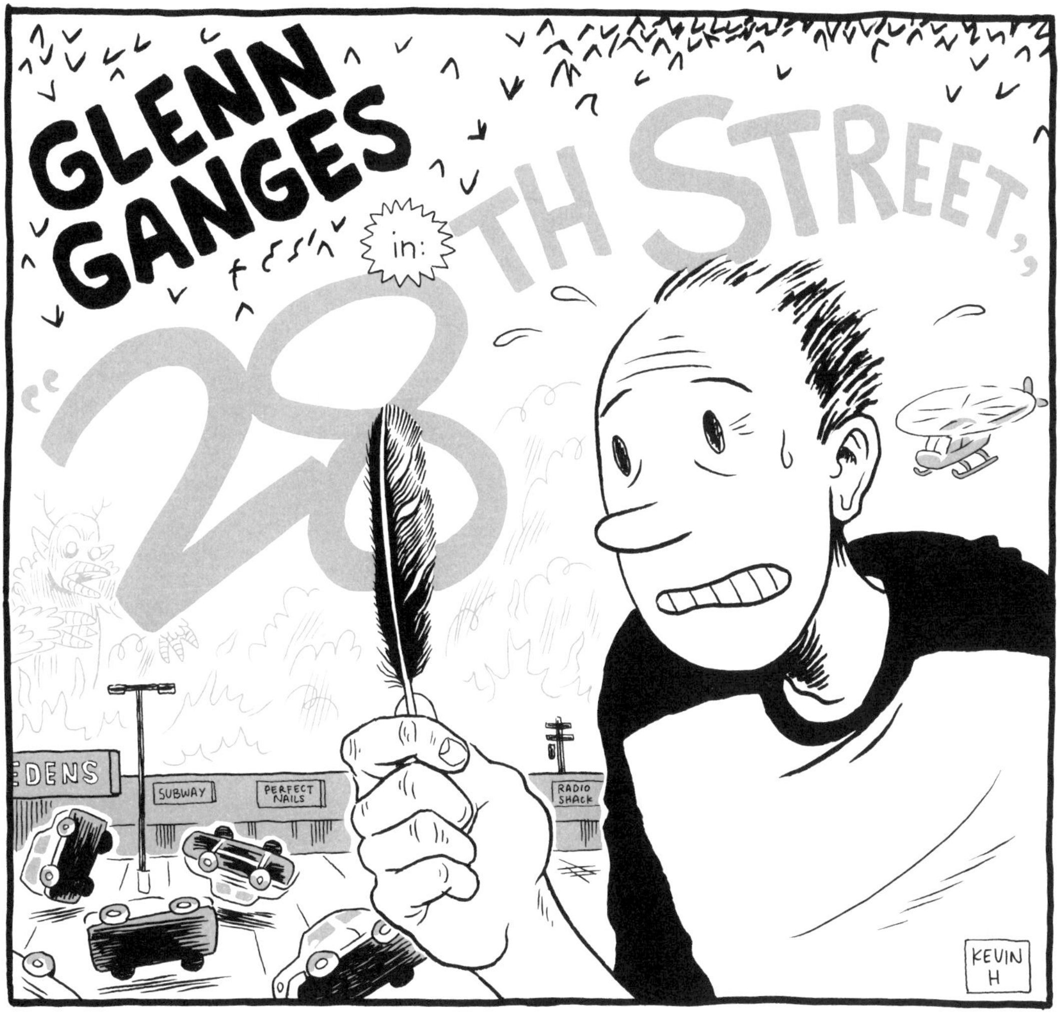
GLENN GANGES
in:
"28TH STREET,"
EDENS
SUBWAY
PERFECT NAILS
RADIO SHACK
KEVIN H

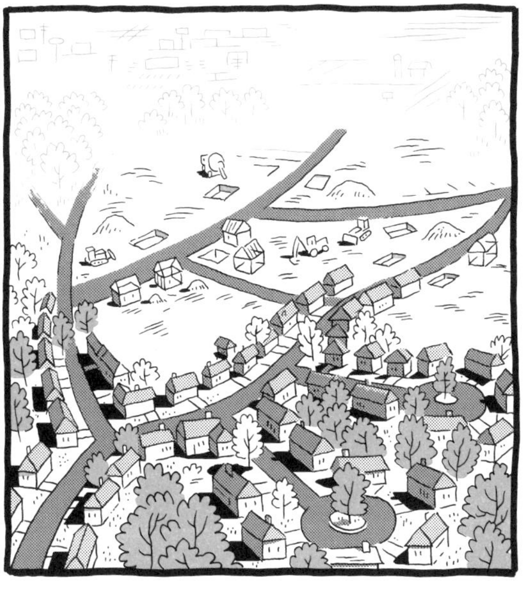

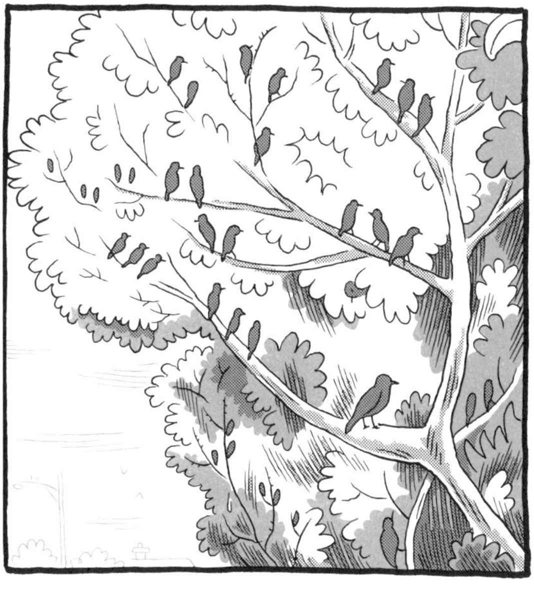

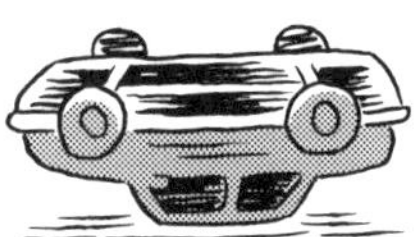

LOOSELY BASED ON
"THE FEATHERED OGRE"
AN ITALIAN FOLKTALE

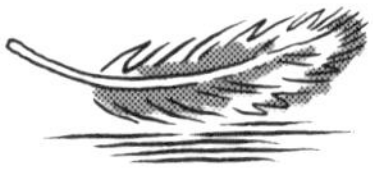

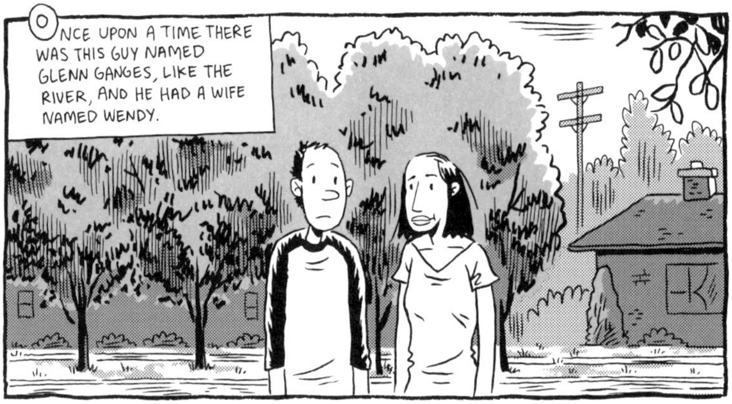
ONCE UPON A TIME THERE WAS THIS GUY NAMED GLENN GANGES, LIKE THE RIVER, AND HE HAD A WIFE NAMED WENDY.

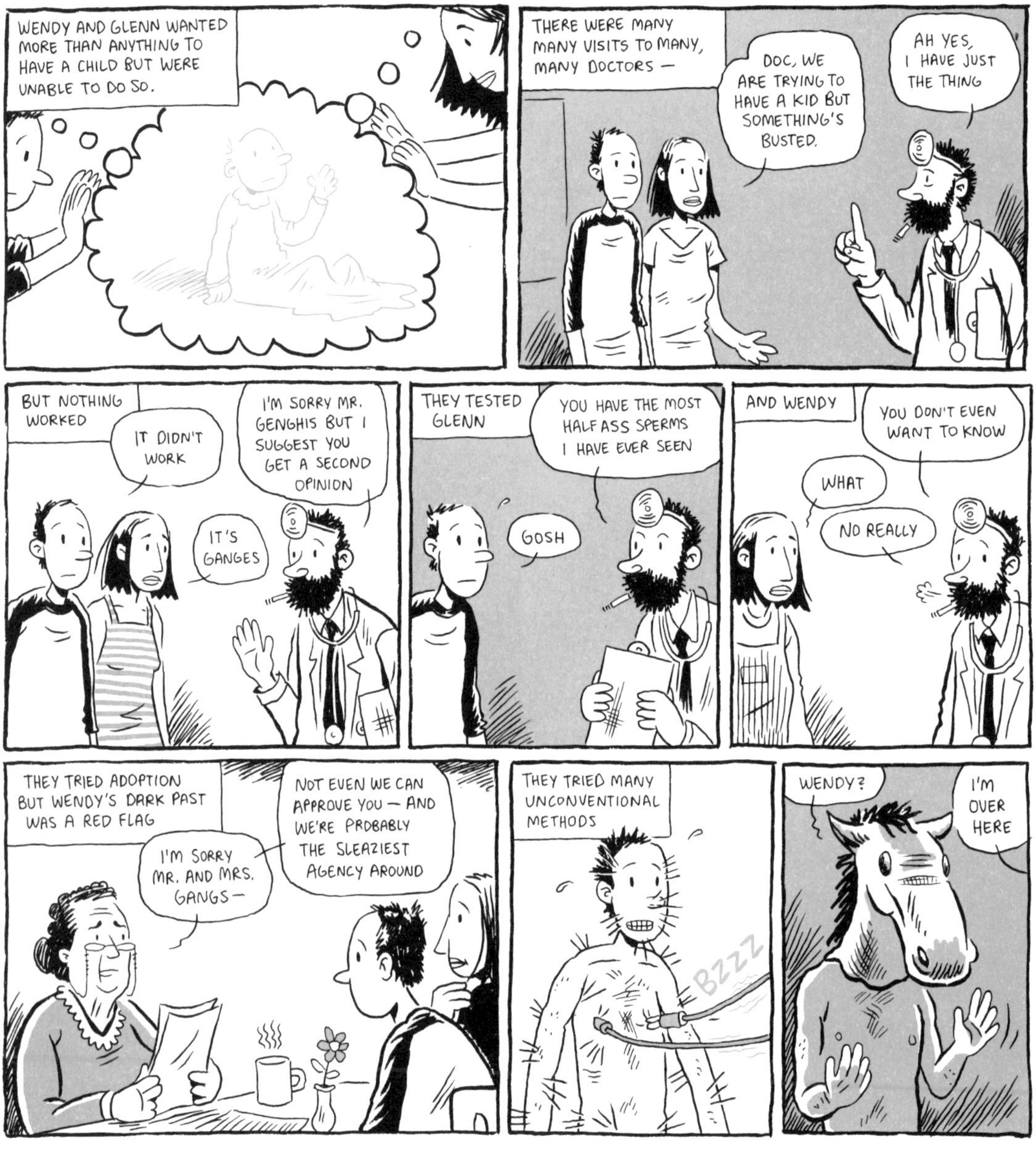
WENDY AND GLENN WANTED MORE THAN ANYTHING TO HAVE A CHILD BUT WERE UNABLE TO DO SO.
THERE WERE MANY MANY VISITS TO MANY, MANY DOCTORS —
DOC, WE ARE TRYING TO HAVE A KID BUT SOMETHING'S BUSTED.
AH YES, I HAVE JUST THE THING
BUT NOTHING WORKED
IT DIDN'T WORK
I'M SORRY MR. GENGHIS BUT I SUGGEST YOU GET A SECOND OPINION
IT'S GANGES
THEY TESTED GLENN
YOU HAVE THE MOST HALF ASS SPERMS I HAVE EVER SEEN
GOSH
AND WENDY
YOU DON'T EVEN WANT TO KNOW
WHAT
NO REALLY
THEY TRIED ADOPTION BUT WENDY'S DARK PAST WAS A RED FLAG
I'M SORRY MR. AND MRS. GANGS—
NOT EVEN WE CAN APPROVE YOU — AND WE'RE PROBABLY THE SLEAZIEST AGENCY AROUND
THEY TRIED MANY UNCONVENTIONAL METHODS
BZZZ
WENDY?
I'M OVER HERE

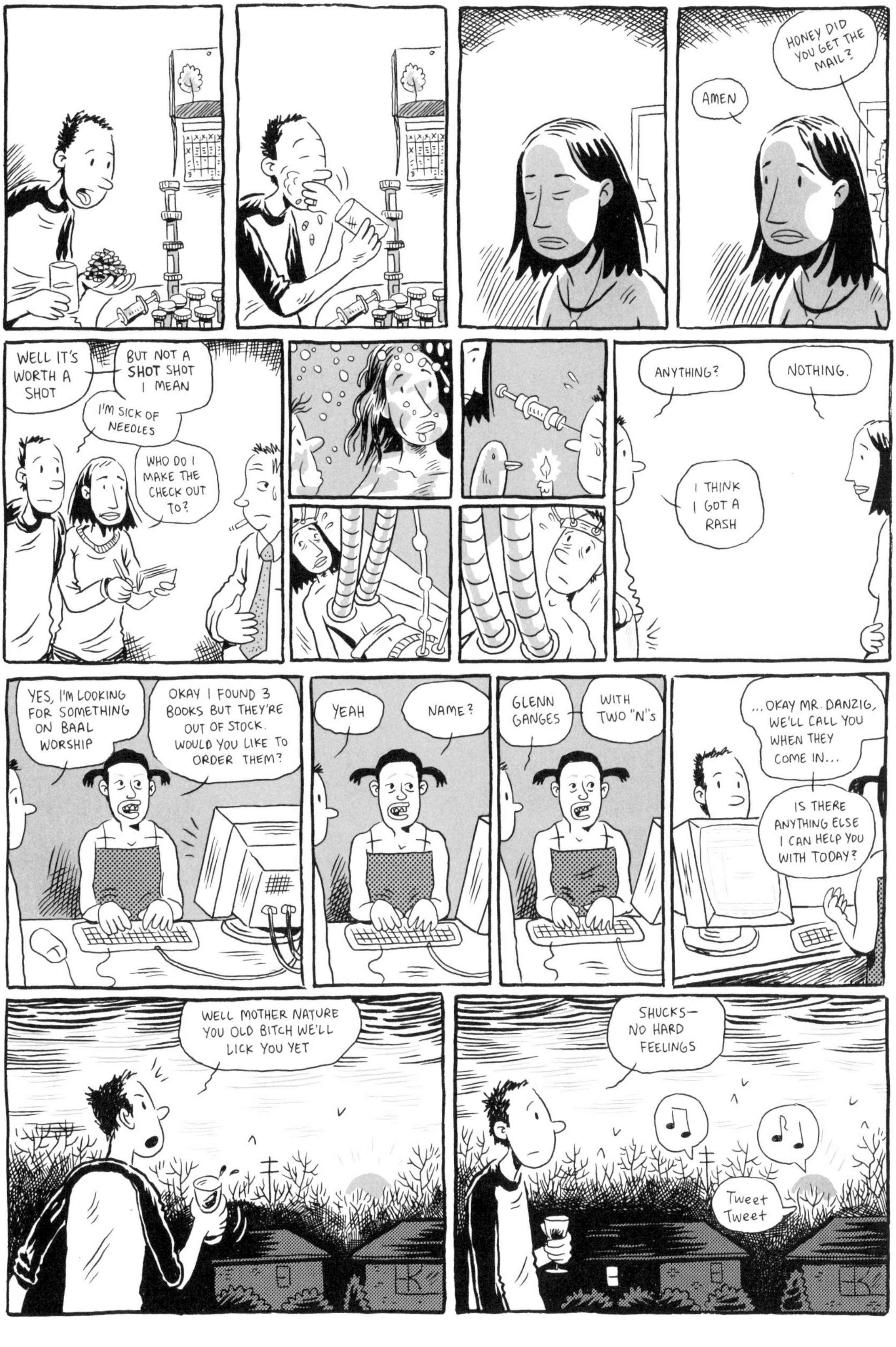
HONEY DID YOU GET THE MAIL?
AMEN
WELL IT'S WORTH A SHOT
BUT NOT A SHOT SHOT I MEAN
I'M SICK OF NEEDLES
WHO DO I MAKE THE CHECK OUT TO?
ANYTHING?
NOTHING.
I THINK I GOT A RASH
YES, I'M LOOKING FOR SOMETHING ON BAAL WORSHIP
OKAY I FOUND 3 BOOKS BUT THEY'RE OUT OF STOCK. WOULD YOU LIKE TO ORDER THEM?
YEAH
NAME?
GLENN GANGES
WITH TWO "N"'s
...OKAY MR. DANZIG, WE'LL CALL YOU WHEN THEY COME IN...
IS THERE ANYTHING ELSE I CAN HELP YOU WITH TODAY?
WELL MOTHER NATURE YOU OLD BITCH WE'LL LICK YOU YET
SHUCKS— NO HARD FEELINGS
Tweet Tweet

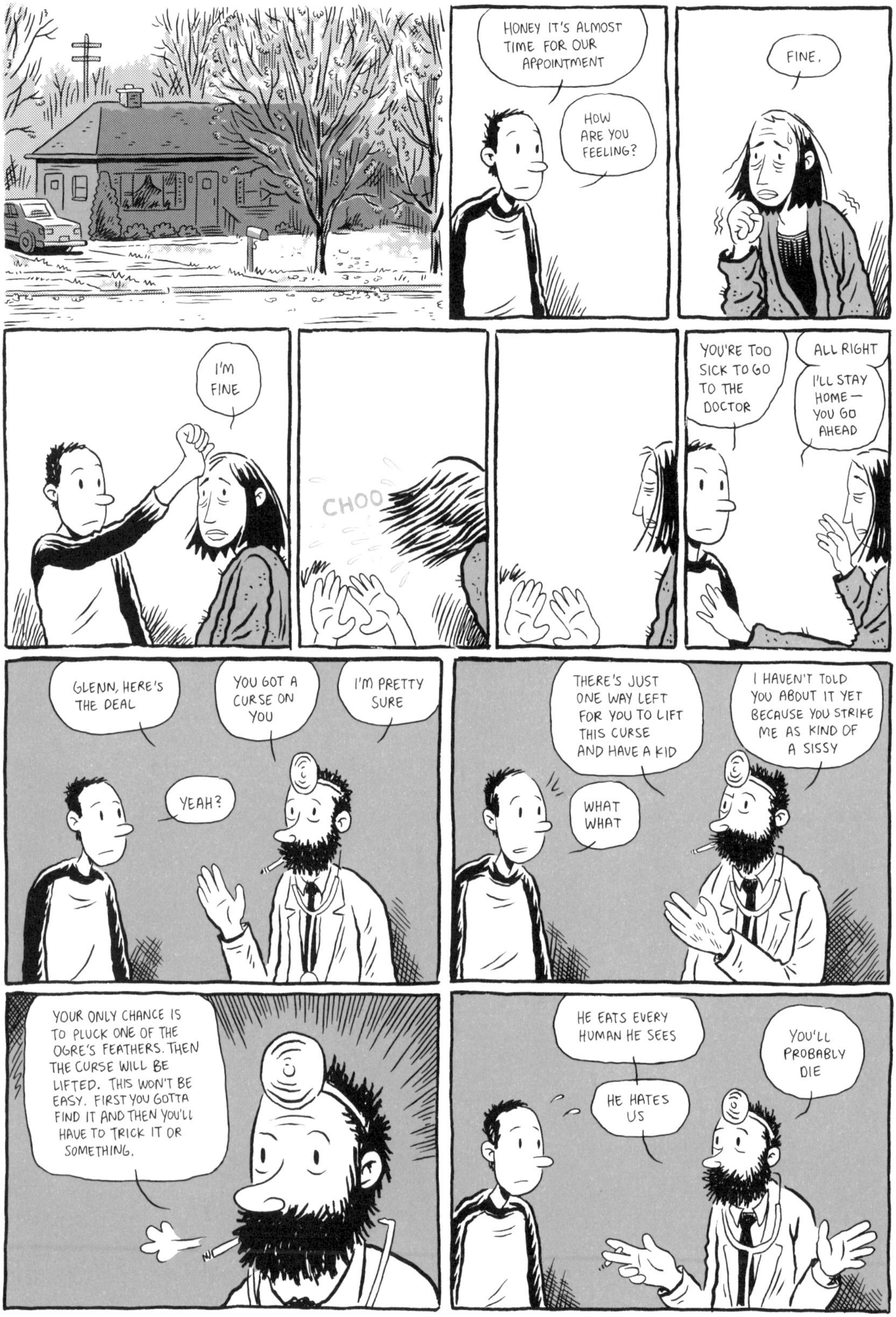
HONEY IT'S ALMOST TIME FOR OUR APPOINTMENT
HOW ARE YOU FEELING?
FINE.
I'M FINE
CHOO
YOU'RE TOO SICK TO GO TO THE DOCTOR
ALL RIGHT
I'LL STAY HOME— YOU GO AHEAD
GLENN, HERE'S THE DEAL
YOU GOT A CURSE ON YOU
I'M PRETTY SURE
YEAH?
THERE'S JUST ONE WAY LEFT FOR YOU TO LIFT THIS CURSE AND HAVE A KID
I HAVEN'T TOLD YOU ABOUT IT YET BECAUSE YOU STRIKE ME AS KIND OF A SISSY
WHAT WHAT
YOUR ONLY CHANCE IS TO PLUCK ONE OF THE OGRE'S FEATHERS. THEN THE CURSE WILL BE LIFTED. THIS WON'T BE EASY. FIRST YOU GOTTA FIND IT AND THEN YOU'LL HAVE TO TRICK IT OR SOMETHING.
HE EATS EVERY HUMAN HE SEES
HE HATES US
YOU'LL PROBABLY DIE

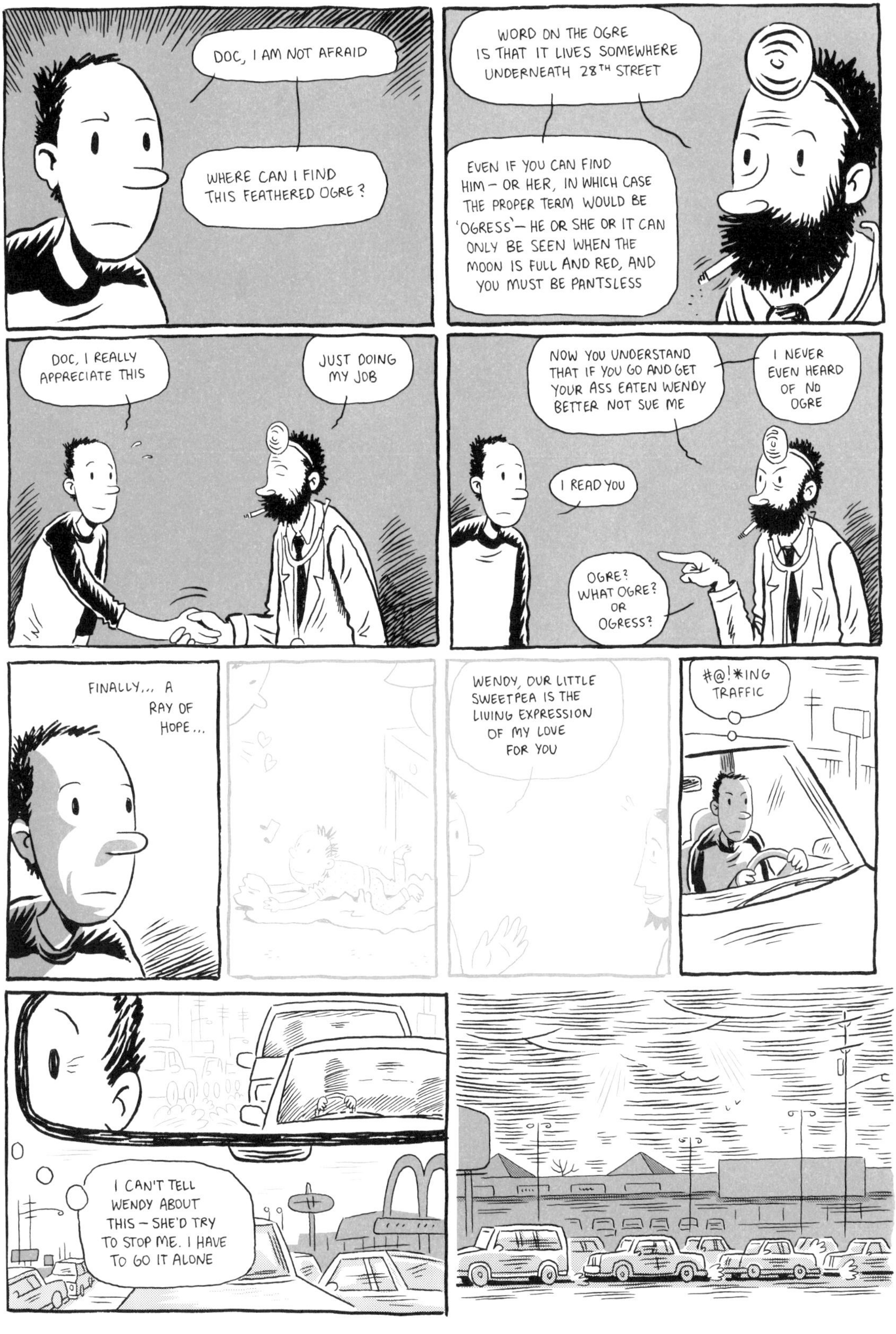
DOC, I AM NOT AFRAID
WHERE CAN I FIND THIS FEATHERED OGRE?
WORD ON THE OGRE IS THAT IT LIVES SOMEWHERE UNDERNEATH 28TH STREET
EVEN IF YOU CAN FIND HIM — OR HER, IN WHICH CASE THE PROPER TERM WOULD BE 'OGRESS'— HE OR SHE OR IT CAN ONLY BE SEEN WHEN THE MOON IS FULL AND RED, AND YOU MUST BE PANTSLESS
DOC, I REALLY APPRECIATE THIS
JUST DOING MY JOB
NOW YOU UNDERSTAND THAT IF YOU GO AND GET YOUR ASS EATEN WENDY BETTER NOT SUE ME
I NEVER EVEN HEARD OF NO OGRE
I READ YOU
OGRE? WHAT OGRE? OR OGRESS?
FINALLY... A RAY OF HOPE...
WENDY, OUR LITTLE SWEETPEA IS THE LIVING EXPRESSION OF MY LOVE FOR YOU
#@!*ING TRAFFIC
I CAN'T TELL WENDY ABOUT THIS — SHE'D TRY TO STOP ME. I HAVE TO GO IT ALONE

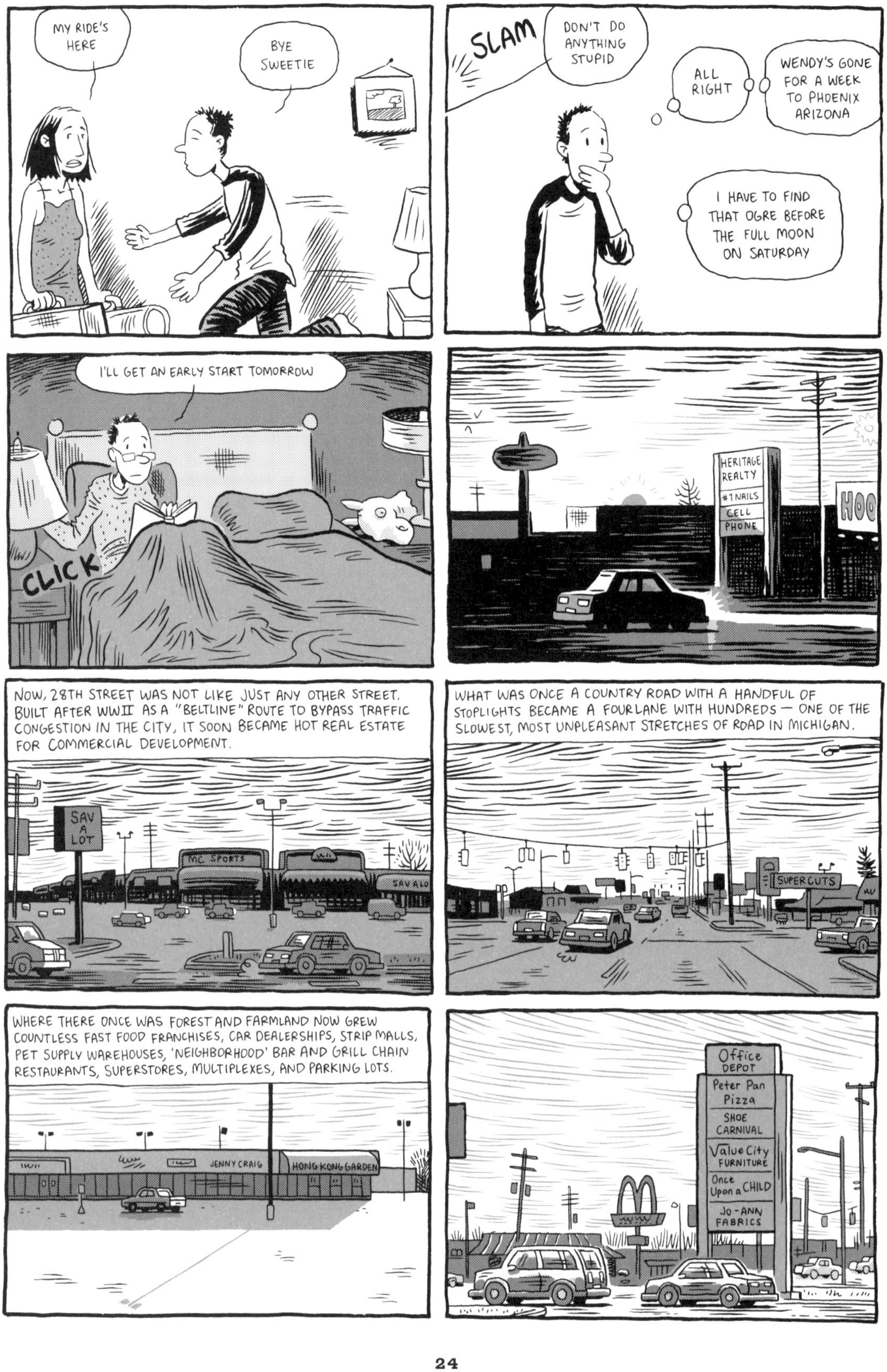
MY RIDE'S HERE
BYE SWEETIE
SLAM
DON'T DO ANYTHING STUPID
ALL RIGHT
WENDY'S GONE FOR A WEEK TO PHOENIX ARIZONA
I HAVE TO FIND THAT OGRE BEFORE THE FULL MOON ON SATURDAY
I'LL GET AN EARLY START TOMORROW
CLICK
HERITAGE REALTY
#1 NAILS
CELL PHONE
NOW, 28TH STREET WAS NOT LIKE JUST ANY OTHER STREET. BUILT AFTER WWII AS A "BELTLINE" ROUTE TO BYPASS TRAFFIC CONGESTION IN THE CITY, IT SOON BECAME HOT REAL ESTATE FOR COMMERCIAL DEVELOPMENT.
SAV A LOT
MC SPORTS
WHAT WAS ONCE A COUNTRY ROAD WITH A HANDFUL OF STOPLIGHTS BECAME A FOURLANE WITH HUNDREDS — ONE OF THE SLOWEST, MOST UNPLEASANT STRETCHES OF ROAD IN MICHIGAN.
SUPERCUTS
WHERE THERE ONCE WAS FOREST AND FARMLAND NOW GREW COUNTLESS FAST FOOD FRANCHISES, CAR DEALERSHIPS, STRIP MALLS, PET SUPPLY WAREHOUSES, 'NEIGHBORHOOD' BAR AND GRILL CHAIN RESTAURANTS, SUPERSTORES, MULTIPLEXES, AND PARKING LOTS.
JENNY CRAIG
HONG KONG GARDEN
Office DEPOT
Peter Pan Pizza
SHOE CARNIVAL
Value City FURNITURE
Once Upon a CHILD
Jo-ANN FABRICS

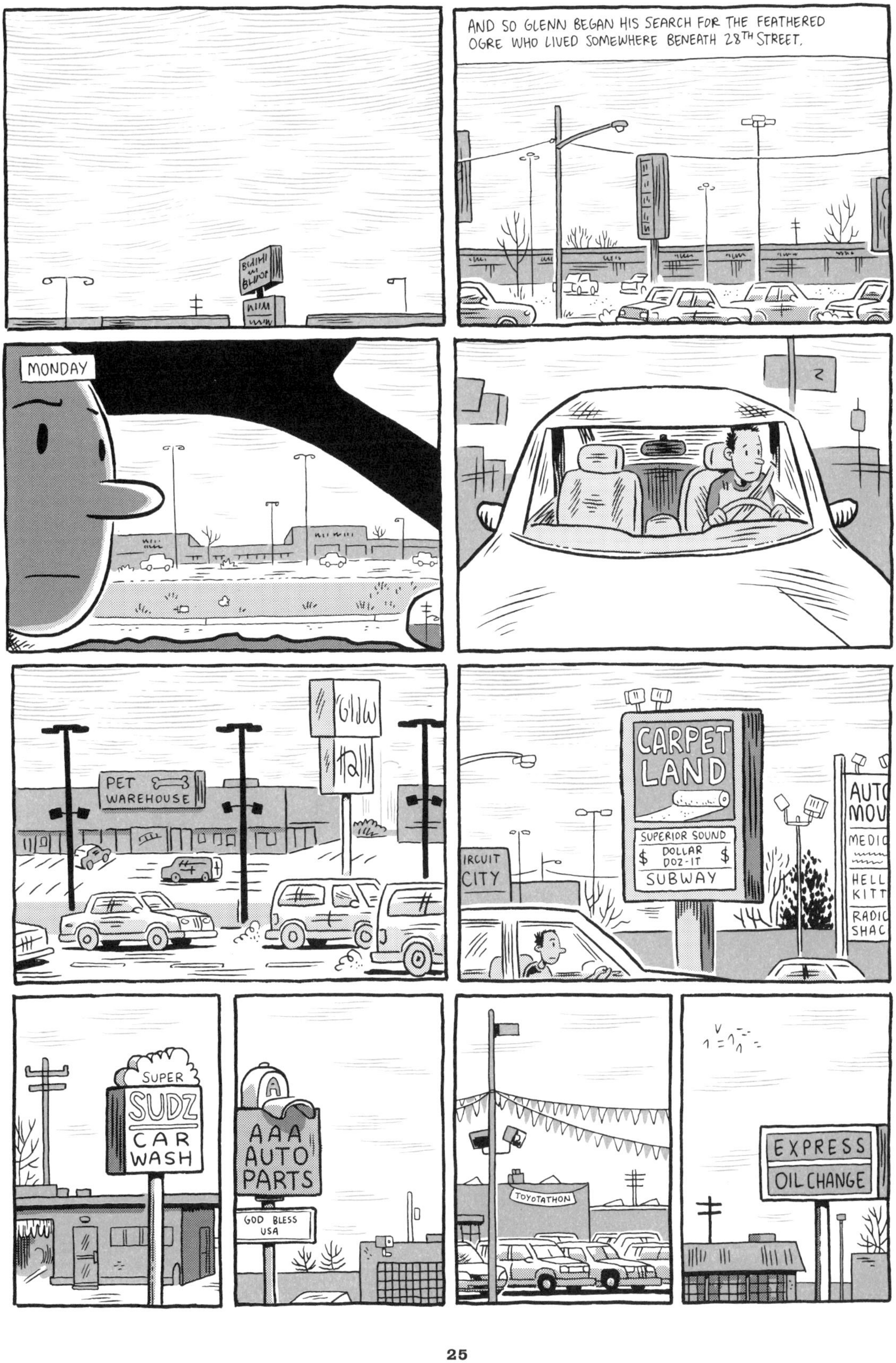
AND SO GLENN BEGAN HIS SEARCH FOR THE FEATHERED OGRE WHO LIVED SOMEWHERE BENEATH 28TH STREET.
MONDAY
PET WAREHOUSE
CARPET LAND
SUPERIOR SOUND
$ DOLLAR DOZ-IT $
SUBWAY
SUPER SUDZ CAR WASH
AAA AUTO PARTS
GOD BLESS USA
TOYOTATHON
EXPRESS OIL CHANGE

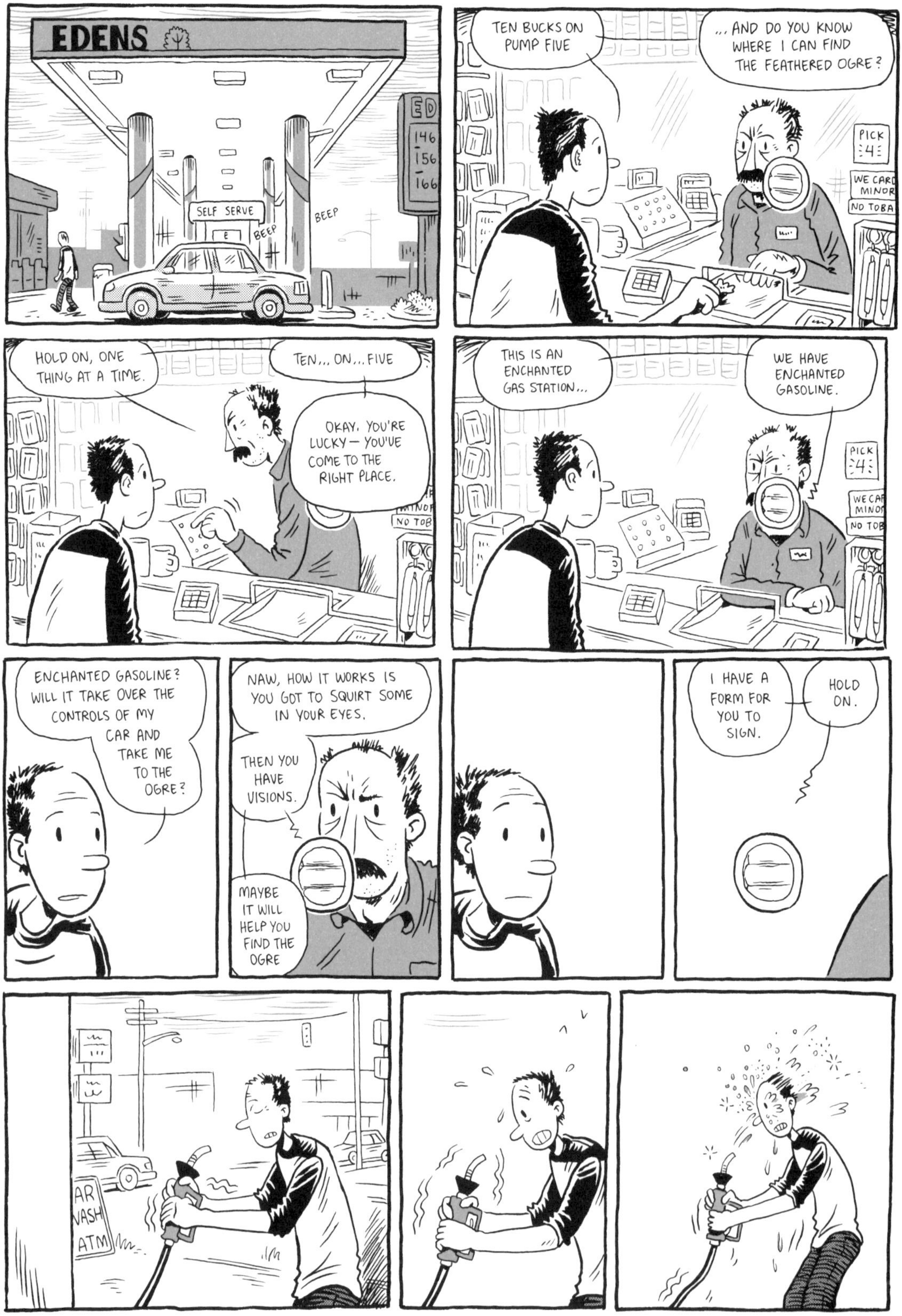
EDENS
SELF SERVE
BEEP
BEEP
TEN BUCKS ON PUMP FIVE
...AND DO YOU KNOW WHERE I CAN FIND THE FEATHERED OGRE?
PICK 4
WE CARD MINOR
NO TOBA
HOLD ON, ONE THING AT A TIME.
TEN... ON... FIVE
OKAY. YOU'RE LUCKY — YOU'VE COME TO THE RIGHT PLACE.
THIS IS AN ENCHANTED GAS STATION...
WE HAVE ENCHANTED GASOLINE.
ENCHANTED GASOLINE? WILL IT TAKE OVER THE CONTROLS OF MY CAR AND TAKE ME TO THE OGRE?
NAW, HOW IT WORKS IS YOU GOT TO SQUIRT SOME IN YOUR EYES.
THEN YOU HAVE VISIONS.
MAYBE IT WILL HELP YOU FIND THE OGRE
I HAVE A FORM FOR YOU TO SIGN.
HOLD ON.
AR WASH ATM

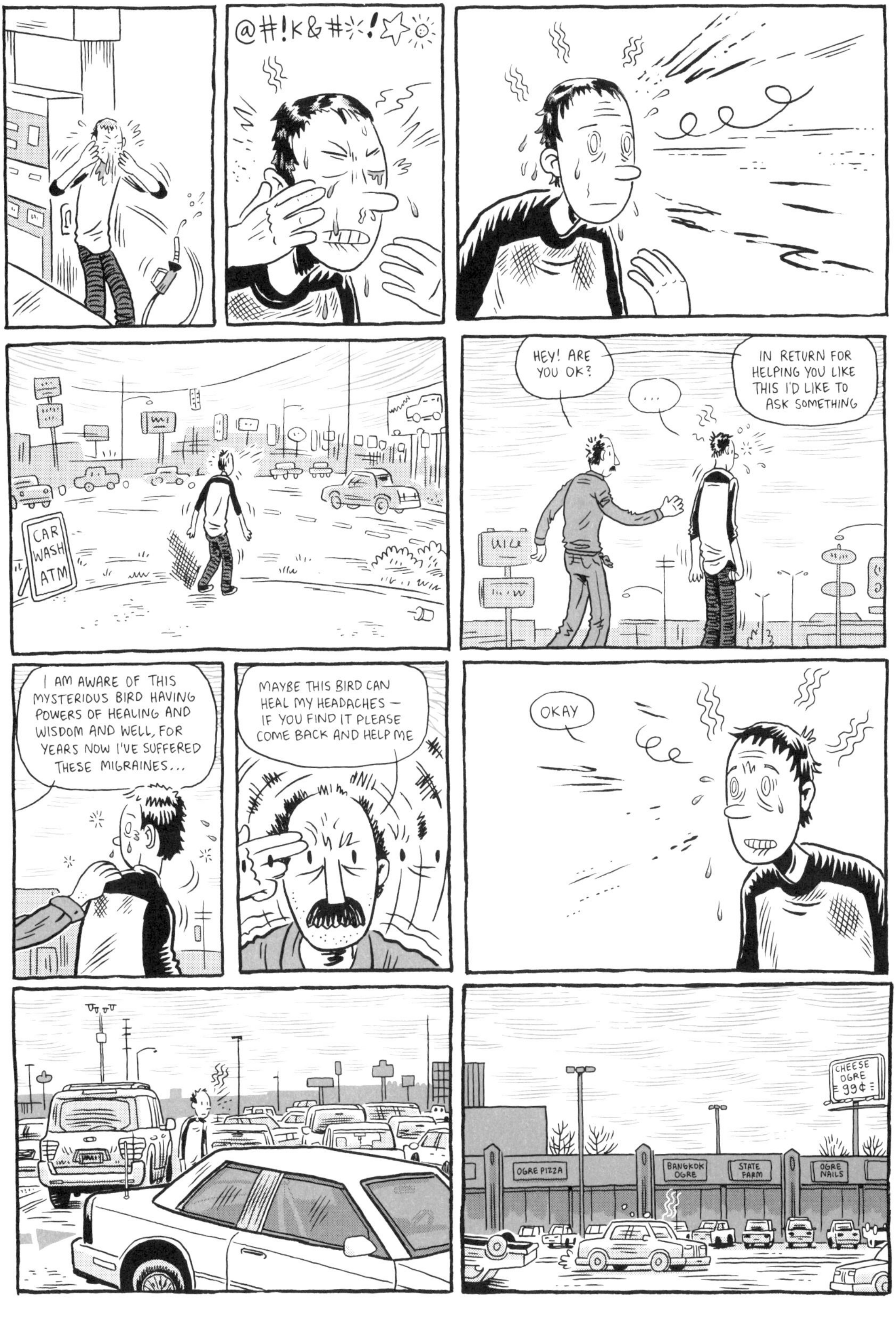

@#!K&#
HEY! ARE YOU OK?
...
IN RETURN FOR HELPING YOU LIKE THIS I'D LIKE TO ASK SOMETHING
CAR WASH ATM
I AM AWARE OF THIS MYSTERIOUS BIRD HAVING POWERS OF HEALING AND WISDOM AND WELL, FOR YEARS NOW I'VE SUFFERED THESE MIGRAINES...
MAYBE THIS BIRD CAN HEAL MY HEADACHES — IF YOU FIND IT PLEASE COME BACK AND HELP ME
OKAY
CHEESE OGRE 99¢
OGRE PIZZA
BANGKOK OGRE
STATE FARM
OGRE NAILS

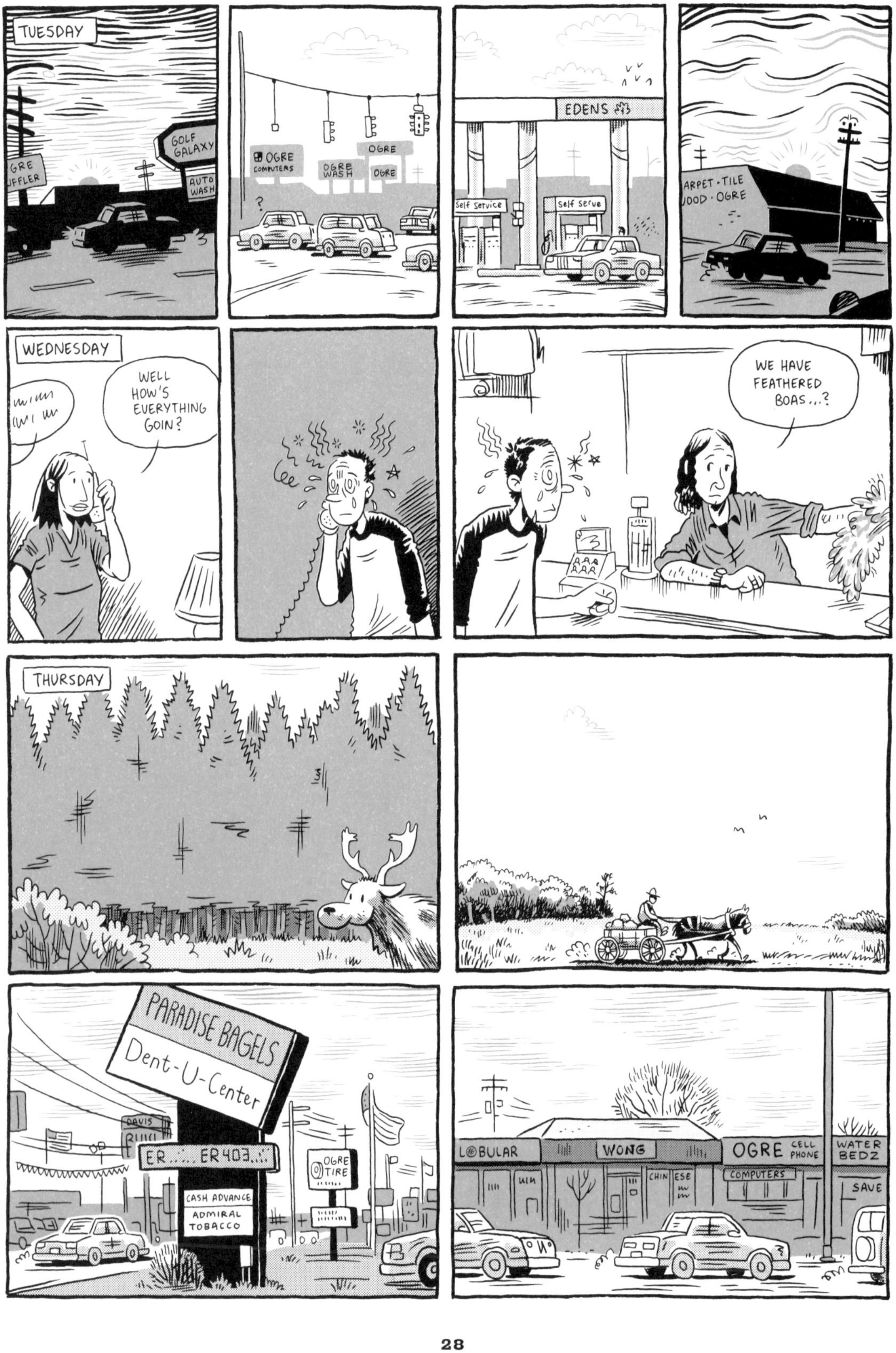
TUESDAY
GRE
UFFLER
GOLF GALAXY
AUTO WASH
OGRE
COMPUTERS
OGRE
OGRE WASH
OGRE
EDENS
Self Service
Self Serve
ARPET · TILE
OOD · OGRE
WEDNESDAY
WELL HOW'S EVERYTHING GOIN?
WE HAVE FEATHERED BOAS...?
THURSDAY
PARADISE BAGELS
Dent-U-Center
DAVIS
ER ER403
CASH ADVANCE
ADMIRAL TOBACCO
OGRE TIRE
L@BULAR
WONG
CHIN ESE
OGRE CELL PHONE
COMPUTERS
WATER BEDZ
SAVE

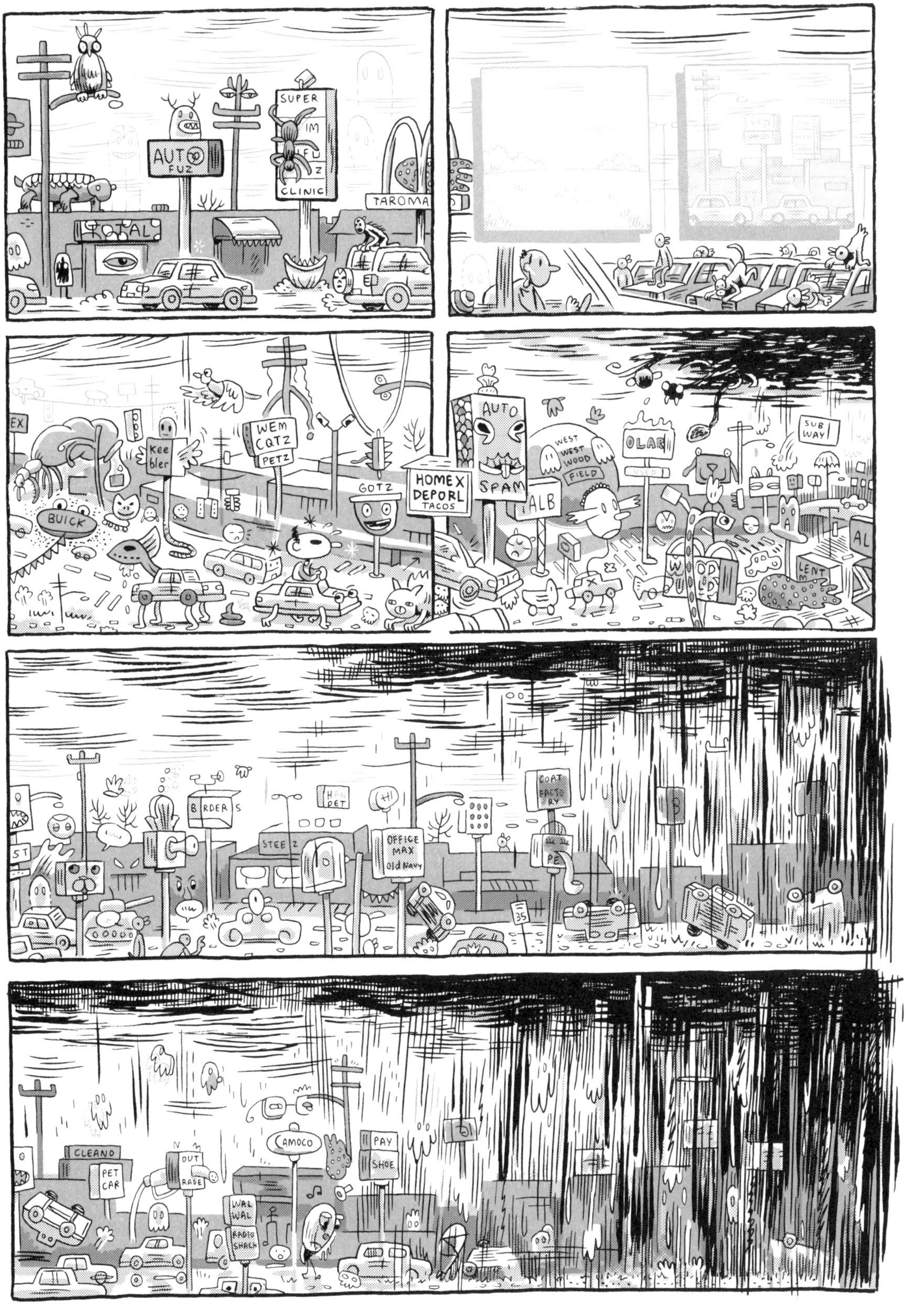
AUTO
FUZ
SUPER
IM
CLINIC
TOTAL
TAROMA
Kee
bler
WEM
CQTZ
PETZ
GOTZ
HOMEX
DEPORL
TACOS
BUICK
AUTO
SPAM
WEST
WEST
WOOD
FIELD
OLAB
SUB
WAY
ALB
LENT
AL
B RDER S
HAN
PET
STEE Z
OFFICE
MAX
Old Navy
COAT
FACTO
RY
35
CLEANO
PET
CAR
OUT
RAGE
CAMOCO
PAY
SHOE
WAL
WAL
RADIO
SHACK

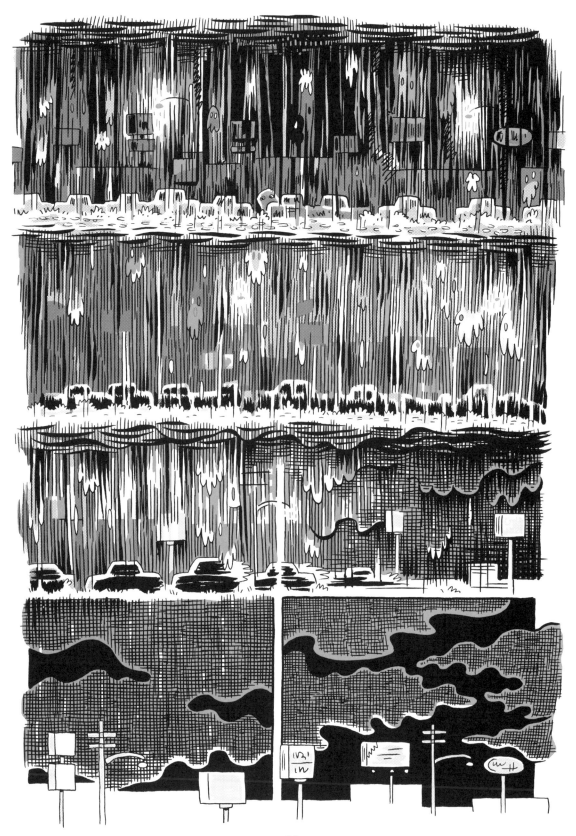

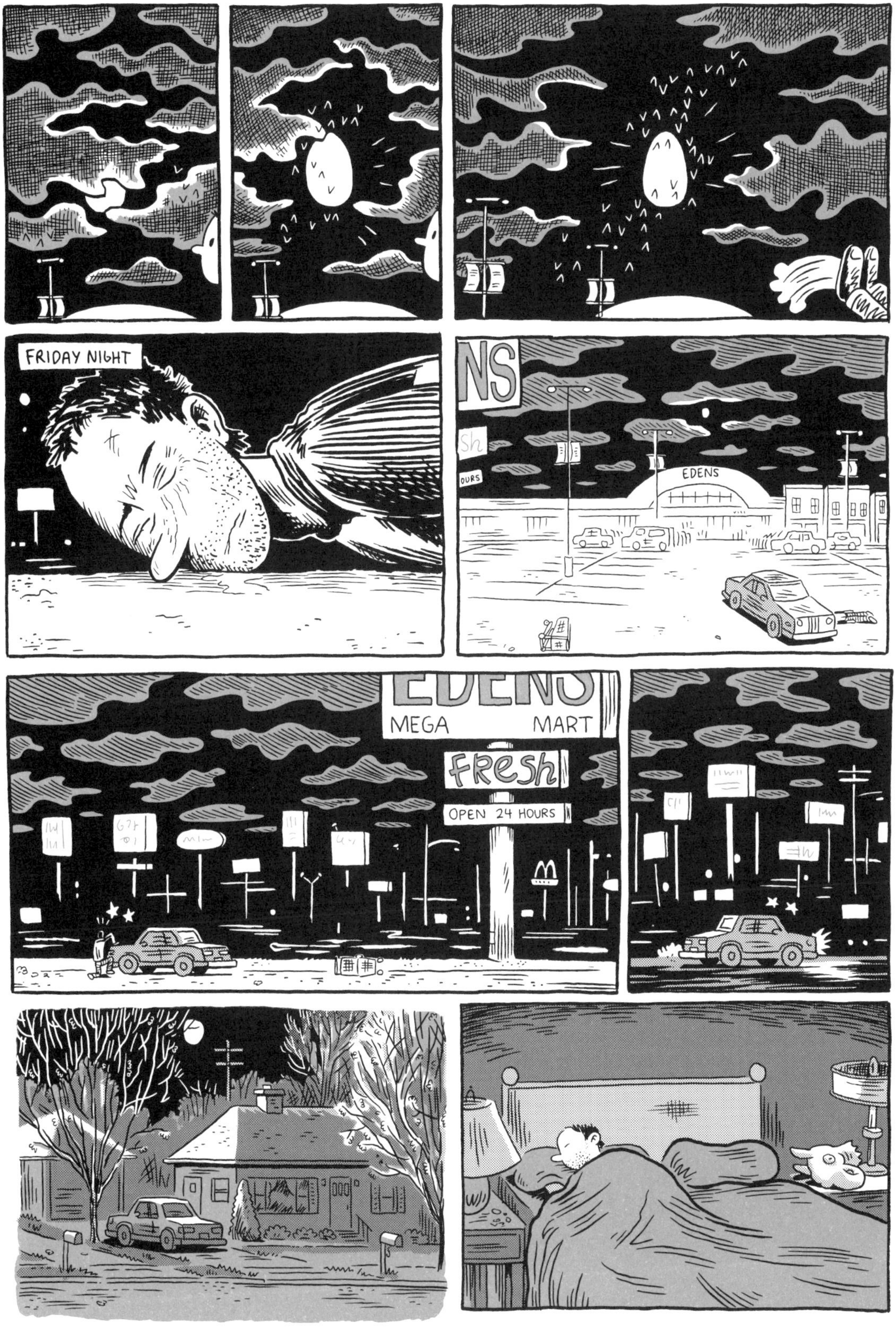
FRIDAY NIGHT
NS
Sh
OURS
EDENS
MEGA MART
fresh
OPEN 24 HOURS

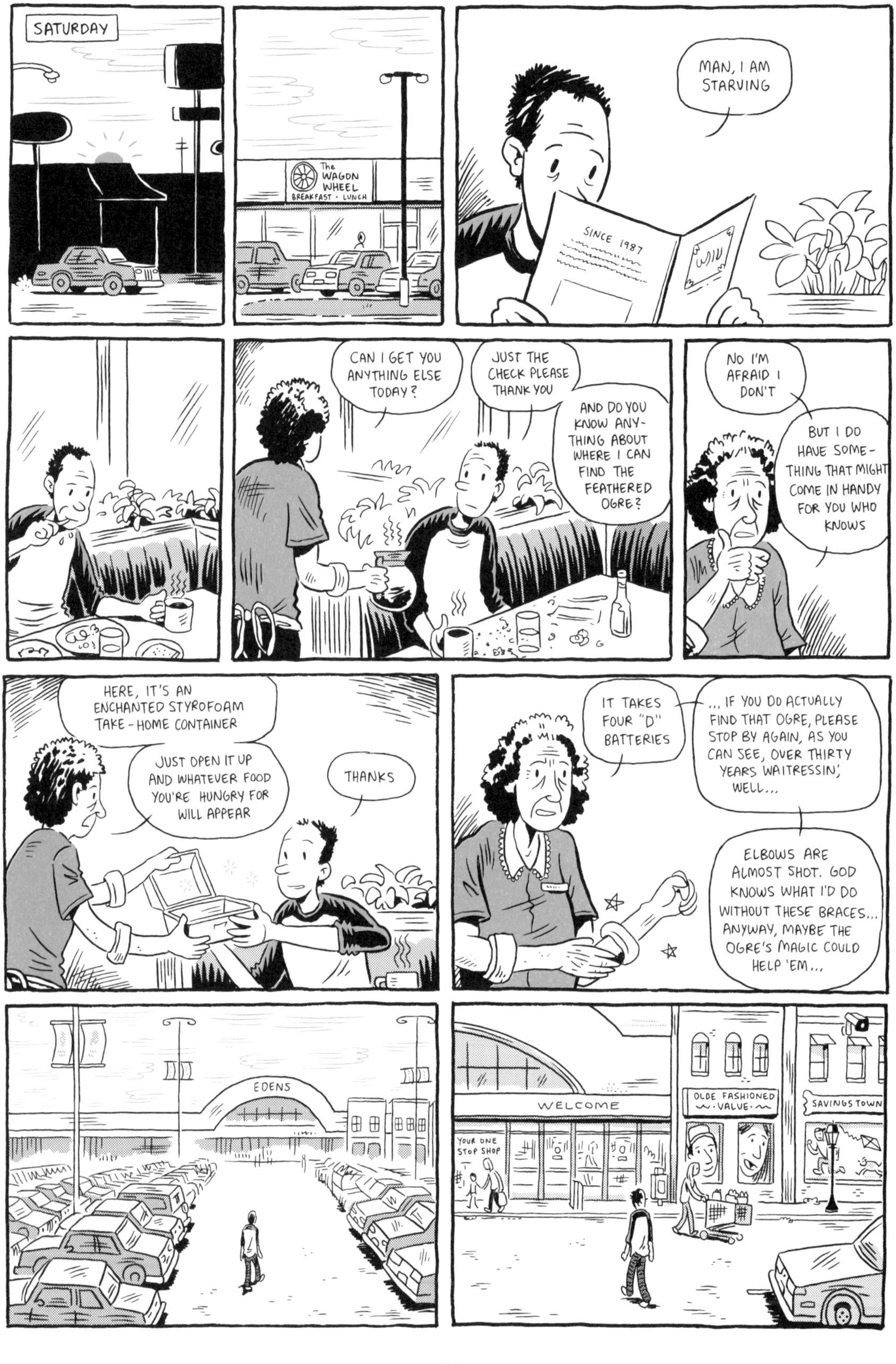
SATURDAY
The WAGON WHEEL BREAKFAST • LUNCH
MAN, I AM STARVING
SINCE 1987
CAN I GET YOU ANYTHING ELSE TODAY?
JUST THE CHECK PLEASE THANK YOU
AND DO YOU KNOW ANYTHING ABOUT WHERE I CAN FIND THE FEATHERED OGRE?
NO I'M AFRAID I DON'T
BUT I DO HAVE SOMETHING THAT MIGHT COME IN HANDY FOR YOU WHO KNOWS
HERE, IT'S AN ENCHANTED STYROFOAM TAKE-HOME CONTAINER
JUST OPEN IT UP AND WHATEVER FOOD YOU'RE HUNGRY FOR WILL APPEAR
THANKS
IT TAKES FOUR "D" BATTERIES
... IF YOU DO ACTUALLY FIND THAT OGRE, PLEASE STOP BY AGAIN, AS YOU CAN SEE, OVER THIRTY YEARS WAITRESSIN', WELL...
ELBOWS ARE ALMOST SHOT. GOD KNOWS WHAT I'D DO WITHOUT THESE BRACES... ANYWAY, MAYBE THE OGRE'S MAGIC COULD HELP 'EM...
EDENS
WELCOME
YOUR ONE STOP SHOP
OLDE FASHIONED VALUE
SAVINGS TOWN

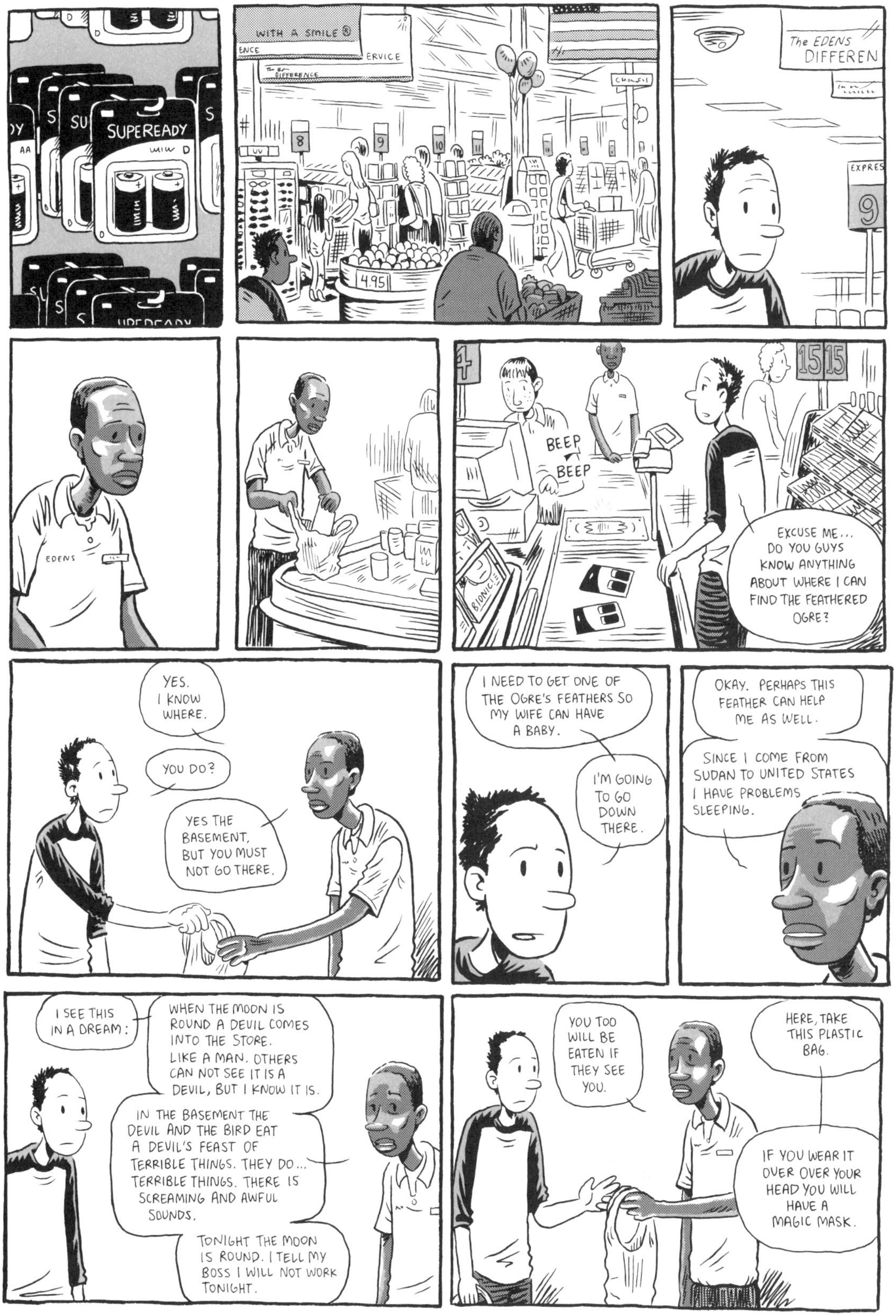
SUPEREADY
WITH A SMILE ®
The EDENS
DIFFEREN
EXPRES
BEEP
BEEP
EXCUSE ME... DO YOU GUYS KNOW ANYTHING ABOUT WHERE I CAN FIND THE FEATHERED OGRE?
YES. I KNOW WHERE.
YOU DO?
YES THE BASEMENT, BUT YOU MUST NOT GO THERE.
I NEED TO GET ONE OF THE OGRE'S FEATHERS SO MY WIFE CAN HAVE A BABY.
I'M GOING TO GO DOWN THERE.
OKAY. PERHAPS THIS FEATHER CAN HELP ME AS WELL.
SINCE I COME FROM SUDAN TO UNITED STATES I HAVE PROBLEMS SLEEPING.
I SEE THIS IN A DREAM:
WHEN THE MOON IS ROUND A DEVIL COMES INTO THE STORE. LIKE A MAN. OTHERS CAN NOT SEE IT IS A DEVIL, BUT I KNOW IT IS.
IN THE BASEMENT THE DEVIL AND THE BIRD EAT A DEVIL'S FEAST OF TERRIBLE THINGS. THEY DO... TERRIBLE THINGS. THERE IS SCREAMING AND AWFUL SOUNDS.
TONIGHT THE MOON IS ROUND. I TELL MY BOSS I WILL NOT WORK TONIGHT.
YOU TOO WILL BE EATEN IF THEY SEE YOU.
HERE, TAKE THIS PLASTIC BAG.
IF YOU WEAR IT OVER OVER YOUR HEAD YOU WILL HAVE A MAGIC MASK.

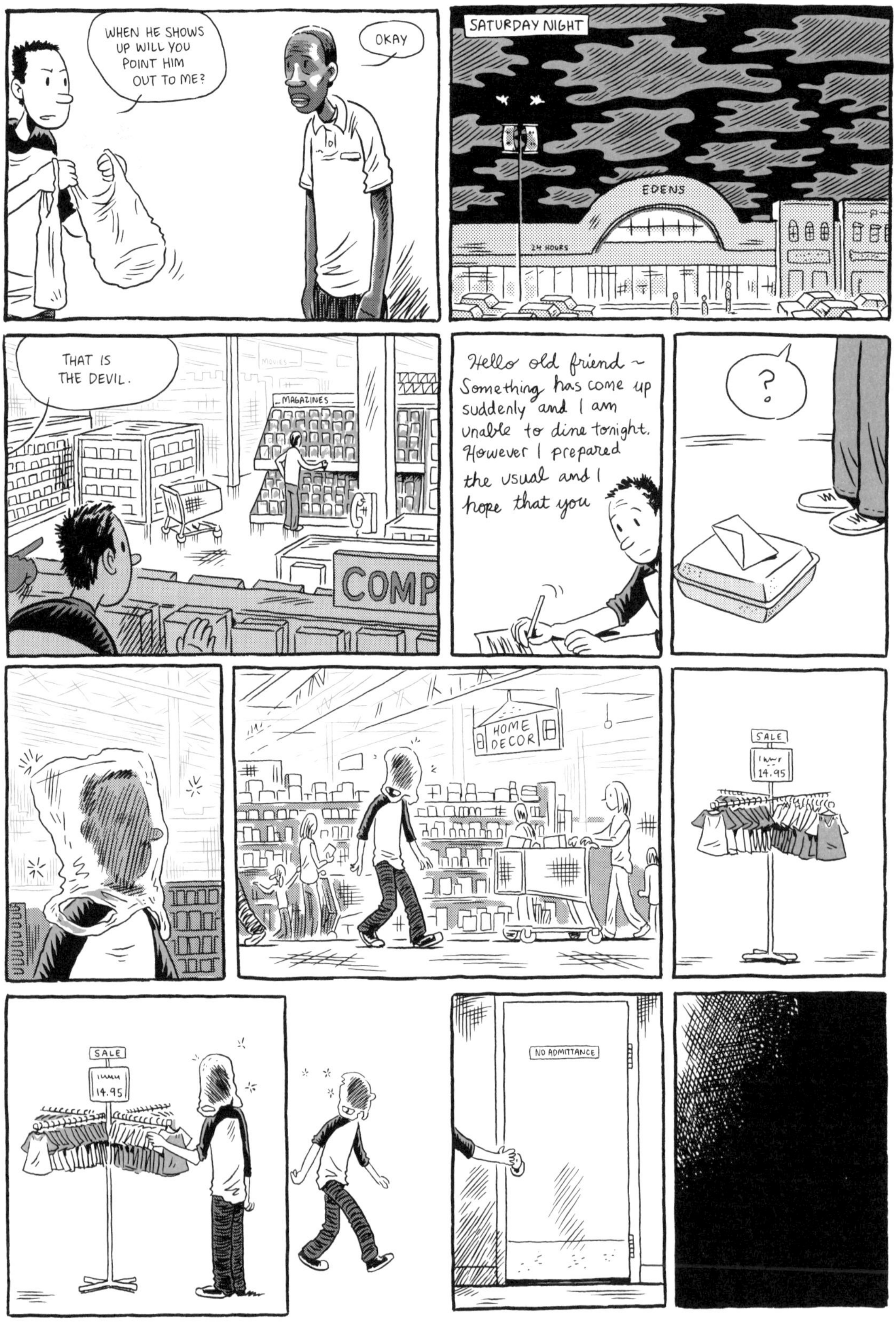

WHEN HE SHOWS UP WILL YOU POINT HIM OUT TO ME?
OKAY
SATURDAY NIGHT
EDENS
24 HOURS
THAT IS THE DEVIL.
MOVIES
MAGAZINES
COMP
Hello old friend ~ Something has come up suddenly and I am unable to dine tonight. However I prepared the usual and I hope that you
?
HOME DECOR
SALE
14.95
SALE
14.95
NO ADMITTANCE

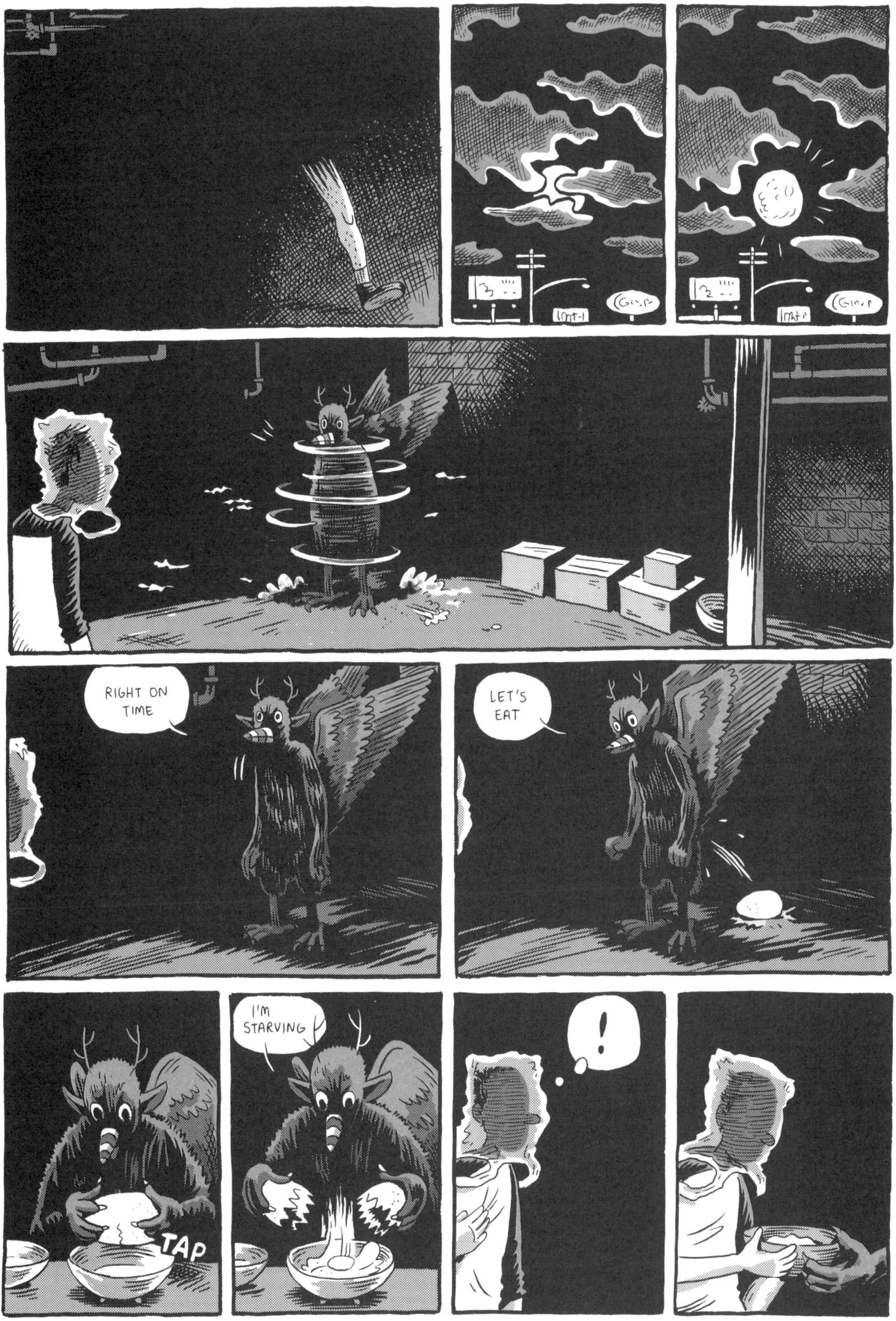
RIGHT ON TIME
LET'S EAT
TAP
I'M STARVING
!

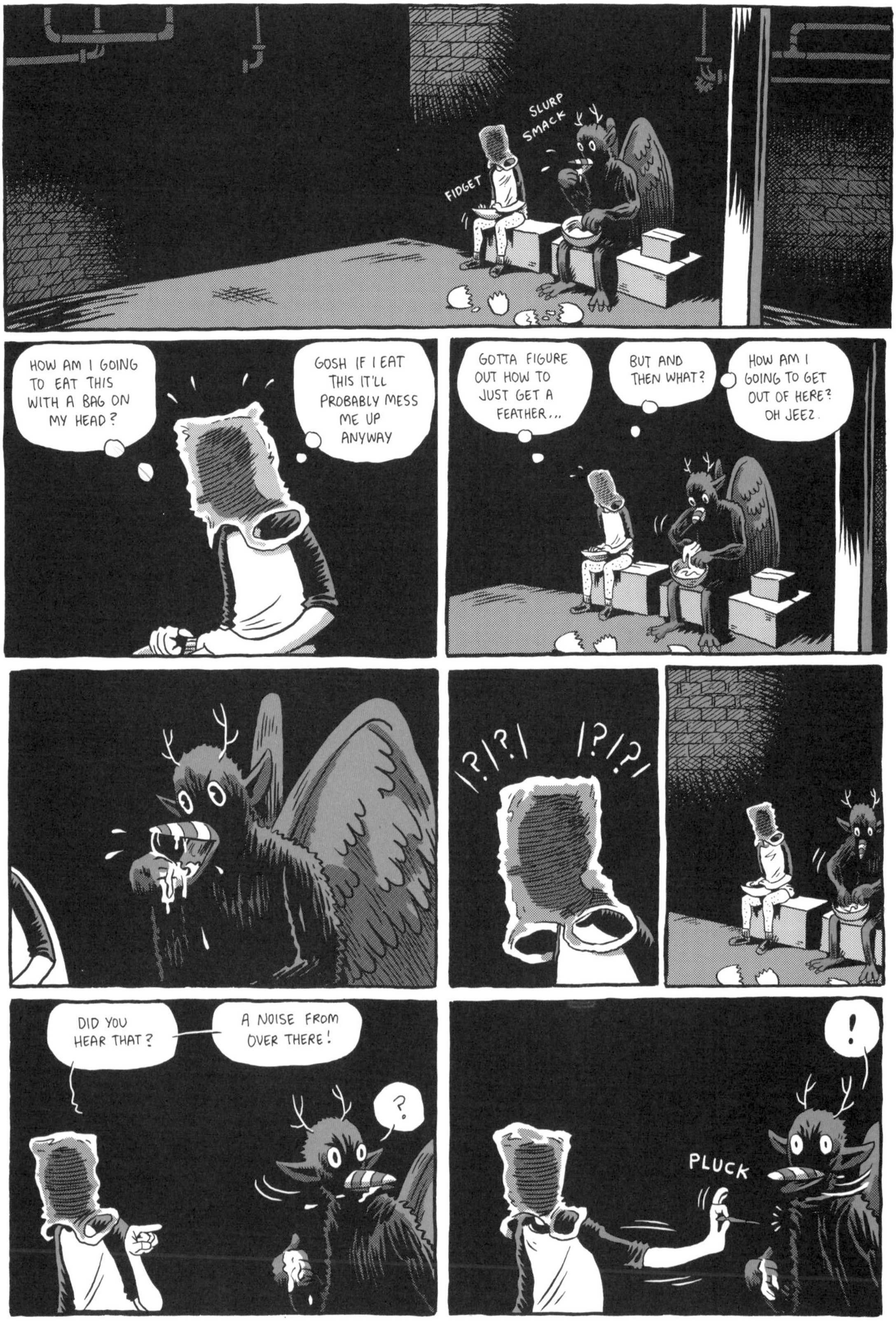
SLURP
SMACK
FIDGET
HOW AM I GOING TO EAT THIS WITH A BAG ON MY HEAD?
GOSH IF I EAT THIS IT'LL PROBABLY MESS ME UP ANYWAY
GOTTA FIGURE OUT HOW TO JUST GET A FEATHER...
BUT AND THEN WHAT?
HOW AM I GOING TO GET OUT OF HERE? OH JEEZ.
!?!?!
!?!?!
DID YOU HEAR THAT?
A NOISE FROM OVER THERE!
?
!
PLUCK

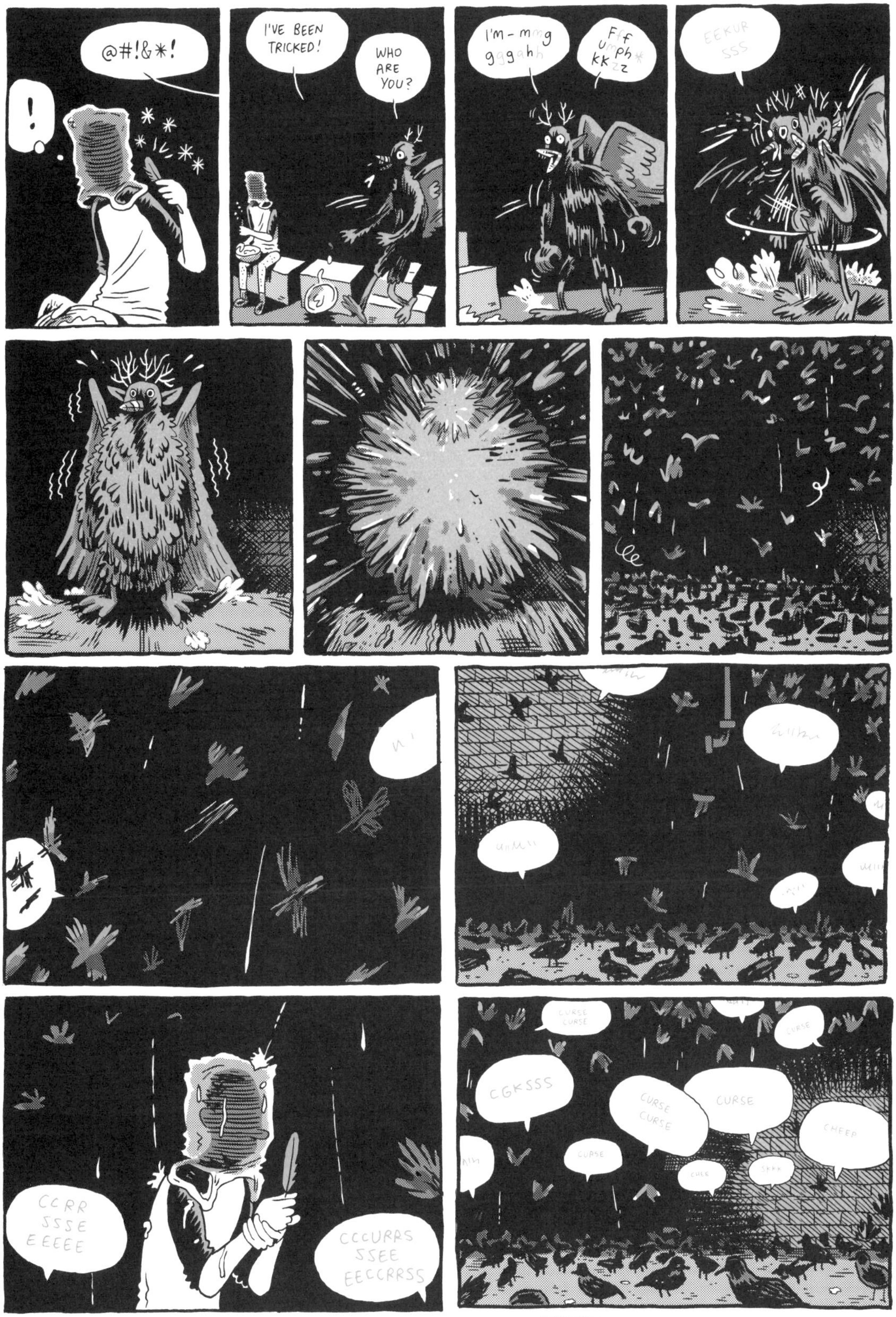
!
@#!&*!
I'VE BEEN TRICKED!
WHO ARE YOU?
I'M-mmg gggahh
Fff umph* kkzz
EEKUR SSS
CCRR SSSE EEEEE
CCCURRS SSEE EECCRRSS
CURSE CURSE
CURSE
CGKSSS
CURSE CURSE
CURSE
CHEEP
CURSE
CHEE
SKKK

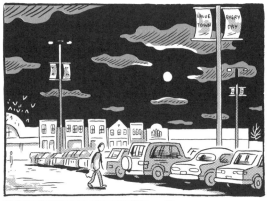

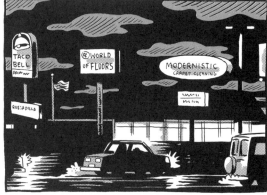

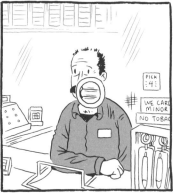

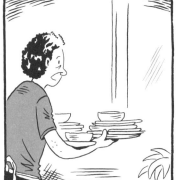

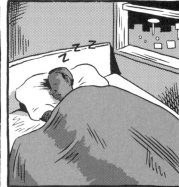

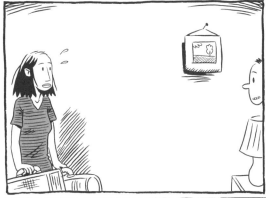

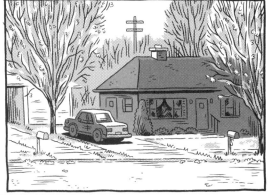

VALUE TOWN
EVERY DAY
TACO BELL
QUESADILLA
WORLD OF FLOORS
MODERNISTIC
CARPET CLEANING
PICK 4
WE CARD MINOR
NO TOBAC
Z Z Z
AND THAT IS HOW GLENN AND WENDY WERE ABLE TO HAVE A BABY.

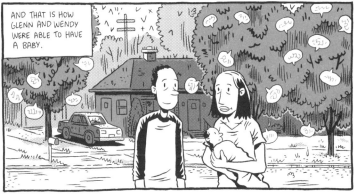

THE END

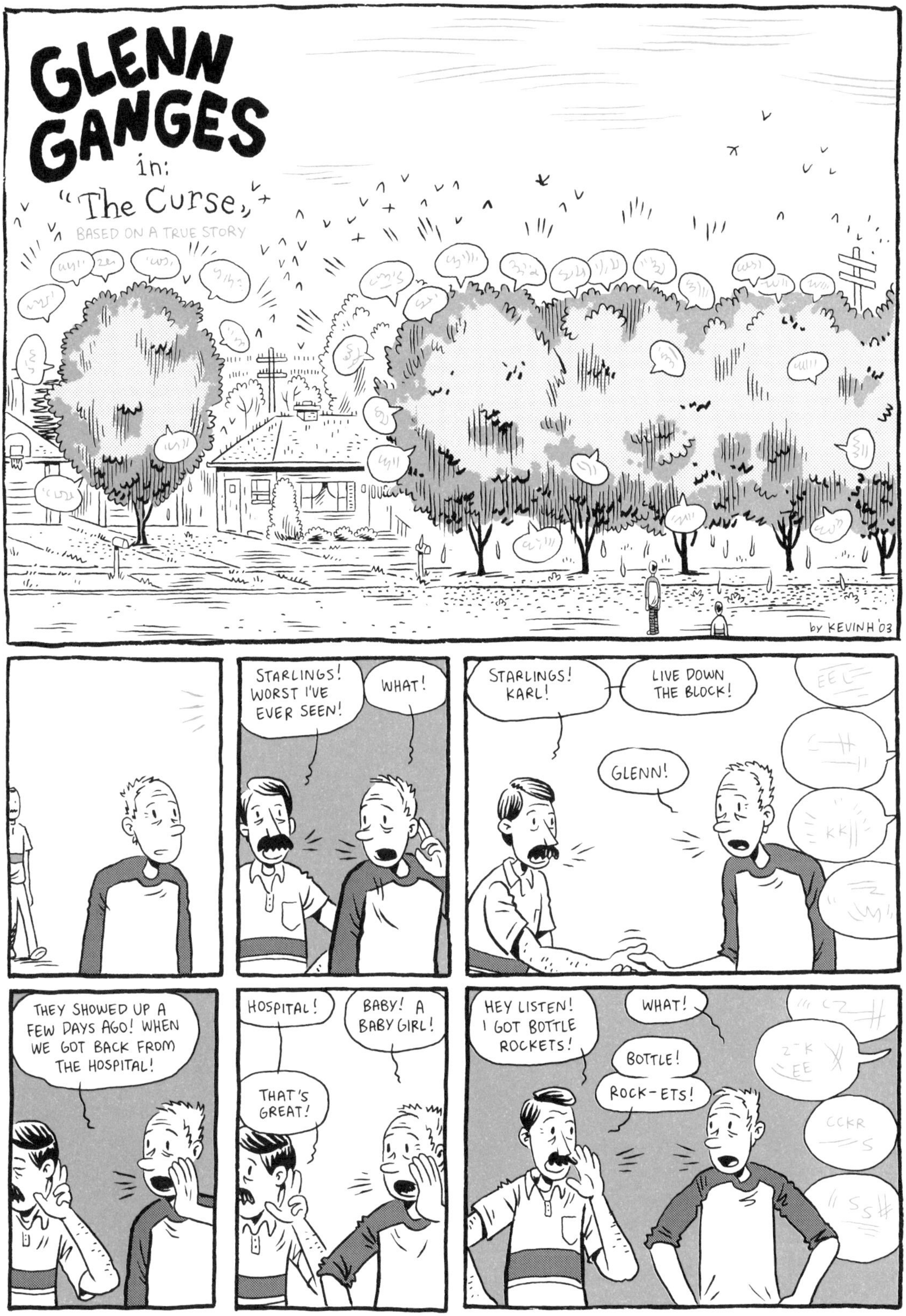
GLENN GANGES
in:
"The Curse,"
BASED ON A TRUE STORY
by KEVINH '03
STARLINGS! WORST I'VE EVER SEEN!
WHAT!
STARLINGS! KARL!
LIVE DOWN THE BLOCK!
GLENN!
THEY SHOWED UP A FEW DAYS AGO! WHEN WE GOT BACK FROM THE HOSPITAL!
HOSPITAL!
BABY! A BABY GIRL!
THAT'S GREAT!
HEY LISTEN! I GOT BOTTLE ROCKETS!
WHAT!
BOTTLE!
ROCK-ETS!

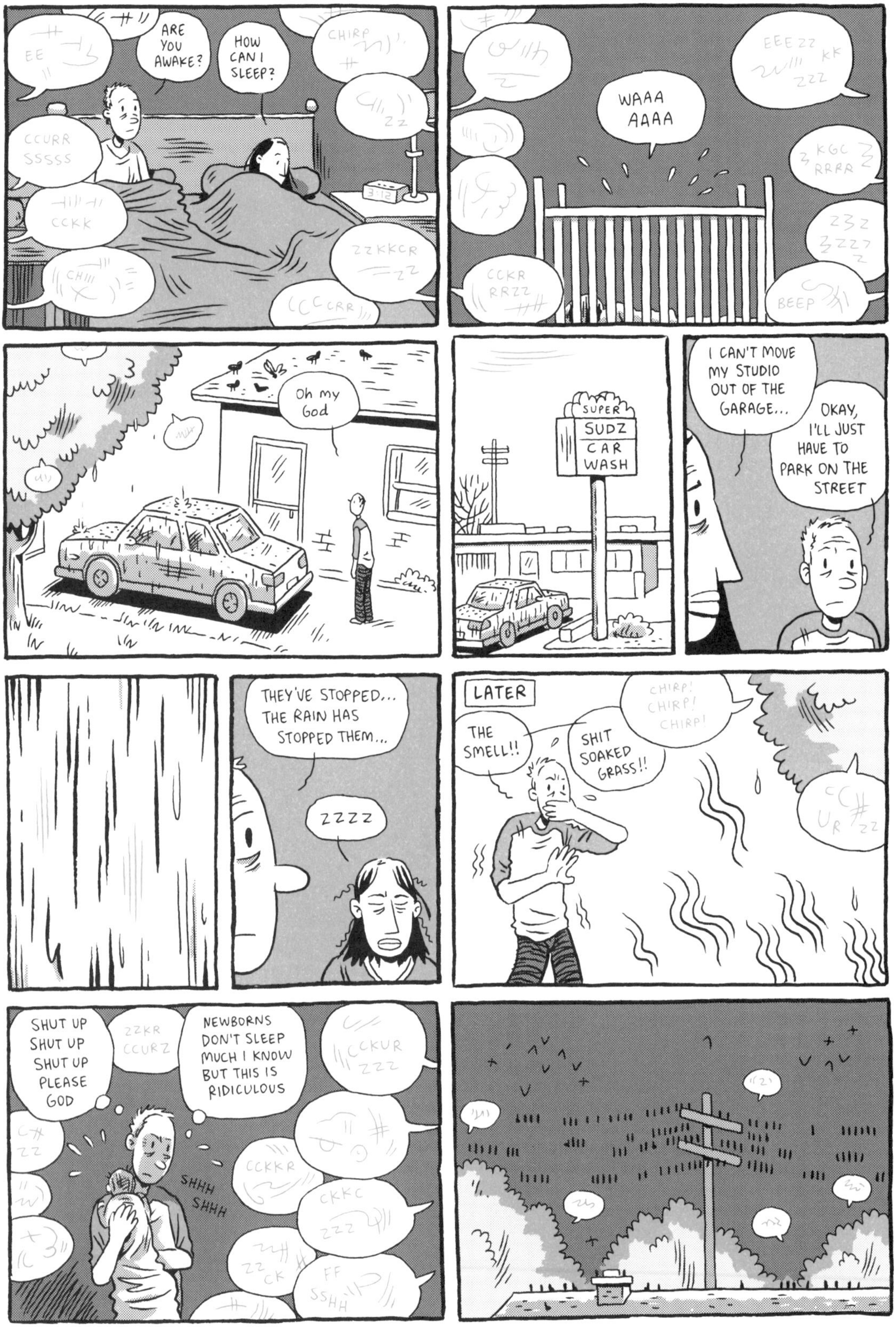
ARE YOU AWAKE?
HOW CAN I SLEEP?
CHIRP
CCURR SSSSS
CCKK
ZZKKCR
CCCCRR
WAAA AAAA
EEEZZ KK ZZZ
ZKGC RRRR
ZZZ ZZZZ
CCKR RRZZ
BEEP
Oh my God
SUPER SUDZ CAR WASH
I CAN'T MOVE MY STUDIO OUT OF THE GARAGE...
OKAY, I'LL JUST HAVE TO PARK ON THE STREET
THEY'VE STOPPED... THE RAIN HAS STOPPED THEM...
ZZZZ
LATER
THE SMELL!!
SHIT SOAKED GRASS!!
CHIRP! CHIRP! CHIRP!
SHUT UP SHUT UP SHUT UP PLEASE GOD
ZZKR CCURZ
NEWBORNS DON'T SLEEP MUCH I KNOW BUT THIS IS RIDICULOUS
CCKUR ZZZ
CCKKR
CKKC ZZZ
SHHH SHHH
ZZ CK
FF SSHH

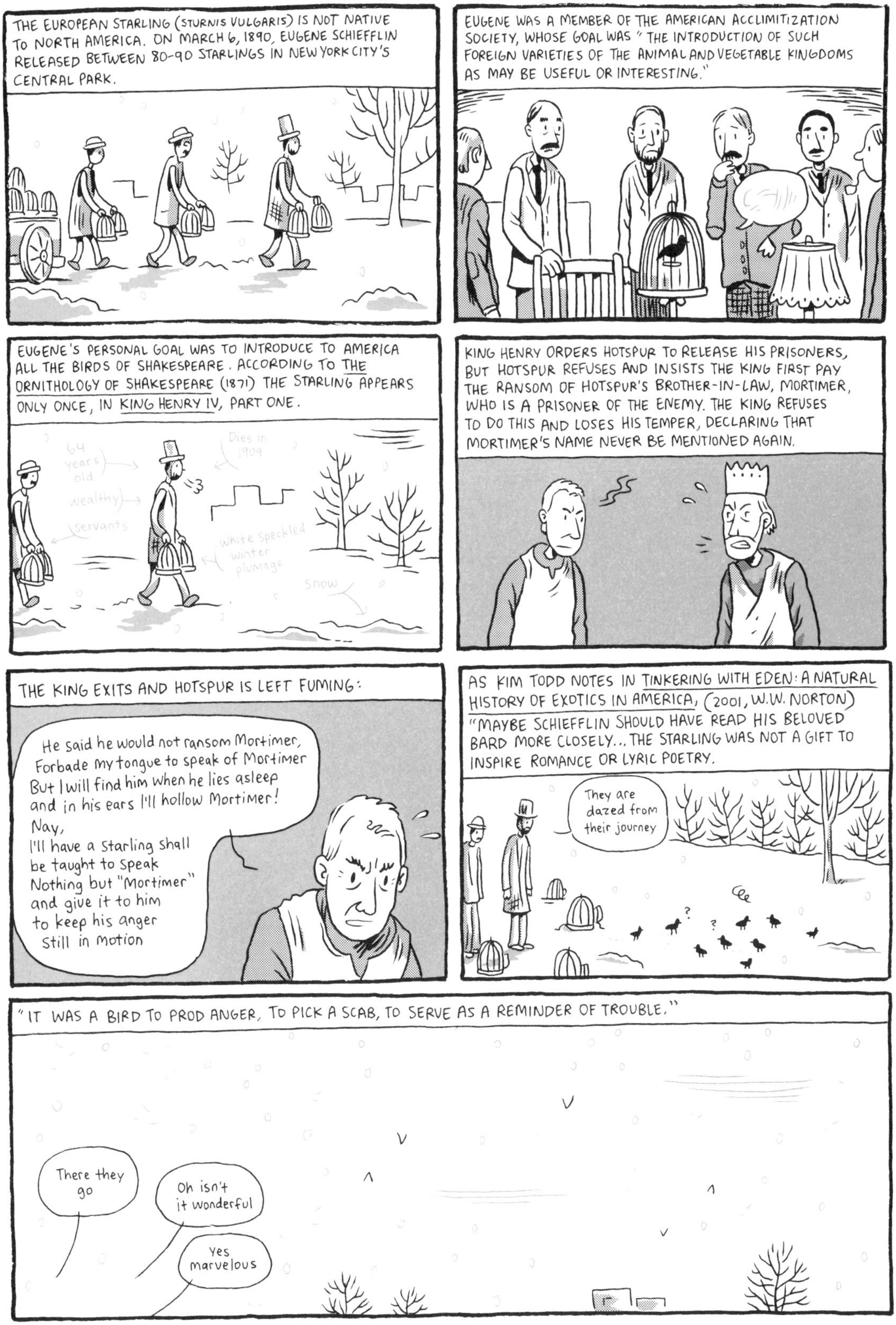
THE EUROPEAN STARLING (STURNIS VULGARIS) IS NOT NATIVE TO NORTH AMERICA. ON MARCH 6, 1890, EUGENE SCHIEFFLIN RELEASED BETWEEN 80-90 STARLINGS IN NEW YORK CITY'S CENTRAL PARK.
EUGENE WAS A MEMBER OF THE AMERICAN ACCLIMITIZATION SOCIETY, WHOSE GOAL WAS "THE INTRODUCTION OF SUCH FOREIGN VARIETIES OF THE ANIMAL AND VEGETABLE KINGDOMS AS MAY BE USEFUL OR INTERESTING."
EUGENE'S PERSONAL GOAL WAS TO INTRODUCE TO AMERICA ALL THE BIRDS OF SHAKESPEARE. ACCORDING TO THE ORNITHOLOGY OF SHAKESPEARE (1871) THE STARLING APPEARS ONLY ONCE, IN KING HENRY IV, PART ONE.
64 years old
Dies in 1909
wealthy
servants
white speckled winter plumage
snow
KING HENRY ORDERS HOTSPUR TO RELEASE HIS PRISONERS, BUT HOTSPUR REFUSES AND INSISTS THE KING FIRST PAY THE RANSOM OF HOTSPUR'S BROTHER-IN-LAW, MORTIMER, WHO IS A PRISONER OF THE ENEMY. THE KING REFUSES TO DO THIS AND LOSES HIS TEMPER, DECLARING THAT MORTIMER'S NAME NEVER BE MENTIONED AGAIN.
THE KING EXITS AND HOTSPUR IS LEFT FUMING:
He said he would not ransom Mortimer, Forbade my tongue to speak of Mortimer But I will find him when he lies asleep and in his ears I'll hollow Mortimer! Nay, I'll have a starling shall be taught to speak Nothing but "Mortimer" and give it to him to keep his anger still in motion
AS KIM TODD NOTES IN TINKERING WITH EDEN: A NATURAL HISTORY OF EXOTICS IN AMERICA, (2001, W.W. NORTON) "MAYBE SCHIEFFLIN SHOULD HAVE READ HIS BELOVED BARD MORE CLOSELY... THE STARLING WAS NOT A GIFT TO INSPIRE ROMANCE OR LYRIC POETRY.
They are dazed from their journey
"IT WAS A BIRD TO PROD ANGER, TO PICK A SCAB, TO SERVE AS A REMINDER OF TROUBLE."
There they go
Oh isn't it wonderful
Yes marvelous

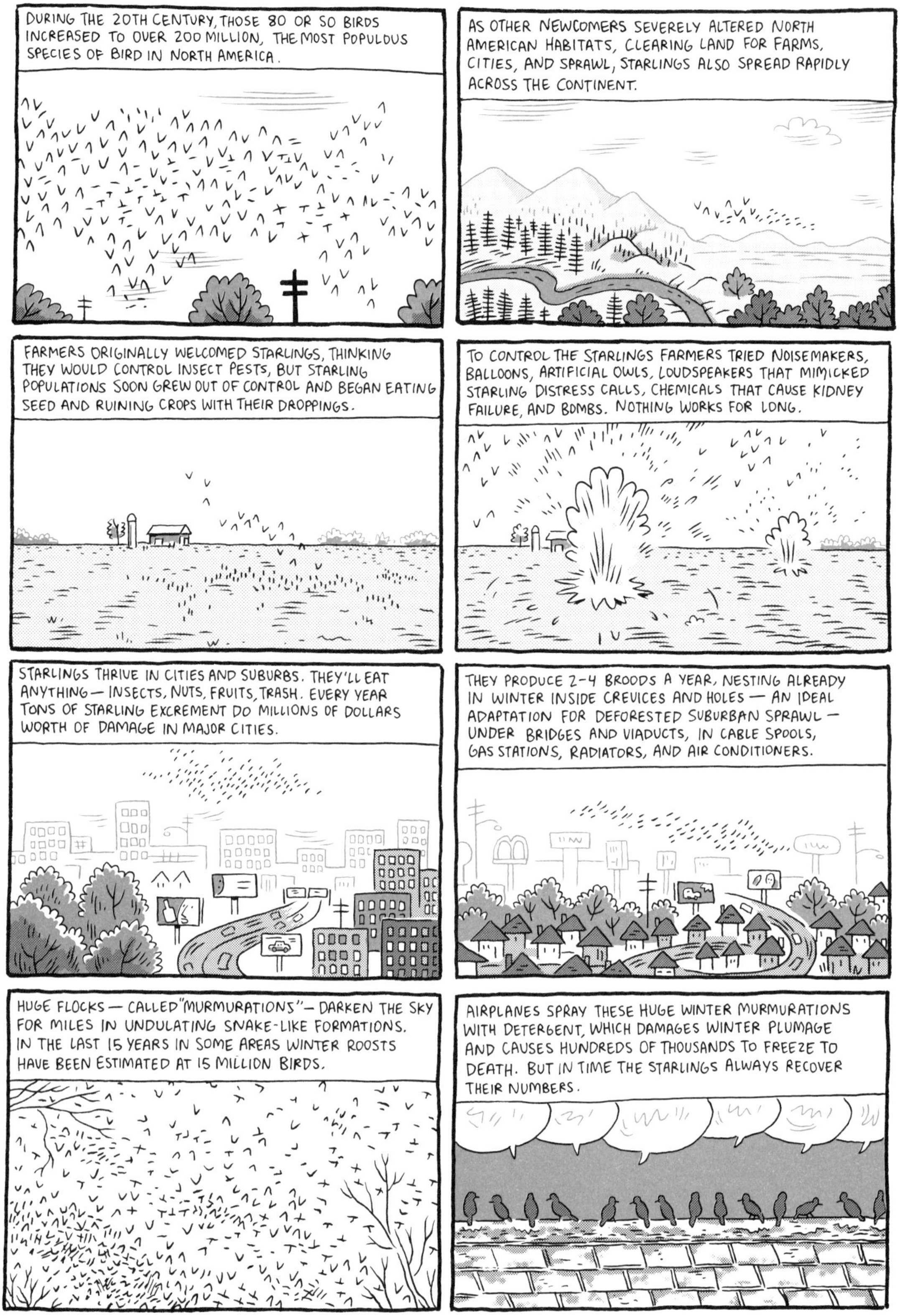
DURING THE 20TH CENTURY, THOSE 80 OR SO BIRDS INCREASED TO OVER 200 MILLION, THE MOST POPULOUS SPECIES OF BIRD IN NORTH AMERICA.
AS OTHER NEWCOMERS SEVERELY ALTERED NORTH AMERICAN HABITATS, CLEARING LAND FOR FARMS, CITIES, AND SPRAWL, STARLINGS ALSO SPREAD RAPIDLY ACROSS THE CONTINENT.
FARMERS ORIGINALLY WELCOMED STARLINGS, THINKING THEY WOULD CONTROL INSECT PESTS, BUT STARLING POPULATIONS SOON GREW OUT OF CONTROL AND BEGAN EATING SEED AND RUINING CROPS WITH THEIR DROPPINGS.
TO CONTROL THE STARLINGS FARMERS TRIED NOISEMAKERS, BALLOONS, ARTIFICIAL OWLS, LOUDSPEAKERS THAT MIMICKED STARLING DISTRESS CALLS, CHEMICALS THAT CAUSE KIDNEY FAILURE, AND BOMBS. NOTHING WORKS FOR LONG.
STARLINGS THRIVE IN CITIES AND SUBURBS. THEY'LL EAT ANYTHING — INSECTS, NUTS, FRUITS, TRASH. EVERY YEAR TONS OF STARLING EXCREMENT DO MILLIONS OF DOLLARS WORTH OF DAMAGE IN MAJOR CITIES.
THEY PRODUCE 2-4 BROODS A YEAR, NESTING ALREADY IN WINTER INSIDE CREVICES AND HOLES — AN IDEAL ADAPTATION FOR DEFORESTED SUBURBAN SPRAWL — UNDER BRIDGES AND VIADUCTS, IN CABLE SPOOLS, GAS STATIONS, RADIATORS, AND AIR CONDITIONERS.
HUGE FLOCKS — CALLED "MURMURATIONS" — DARKEN THE SKY FOR MILES IN UNDULATING SNAKE-LIKE FORMATIONS. IN THE LAST 15 YEARS IN SOME AREAS WINTER ROOSTS HAVE BEEN ESTIMATED AT 15 MILLION BIRDS.
AIRPLANES SPRAY THESE HUGE WINTER MURMURATIONS WITH DETERGENT, WHICH DAMAGES WINTER PLUMAGE AND CAUSES HUNDREDS OF THOUSANDS TO FREEZE TO DEATH. BUT IN TIME THE STARLINGS ALWAYS RECOVER THEIR NUMBERS.

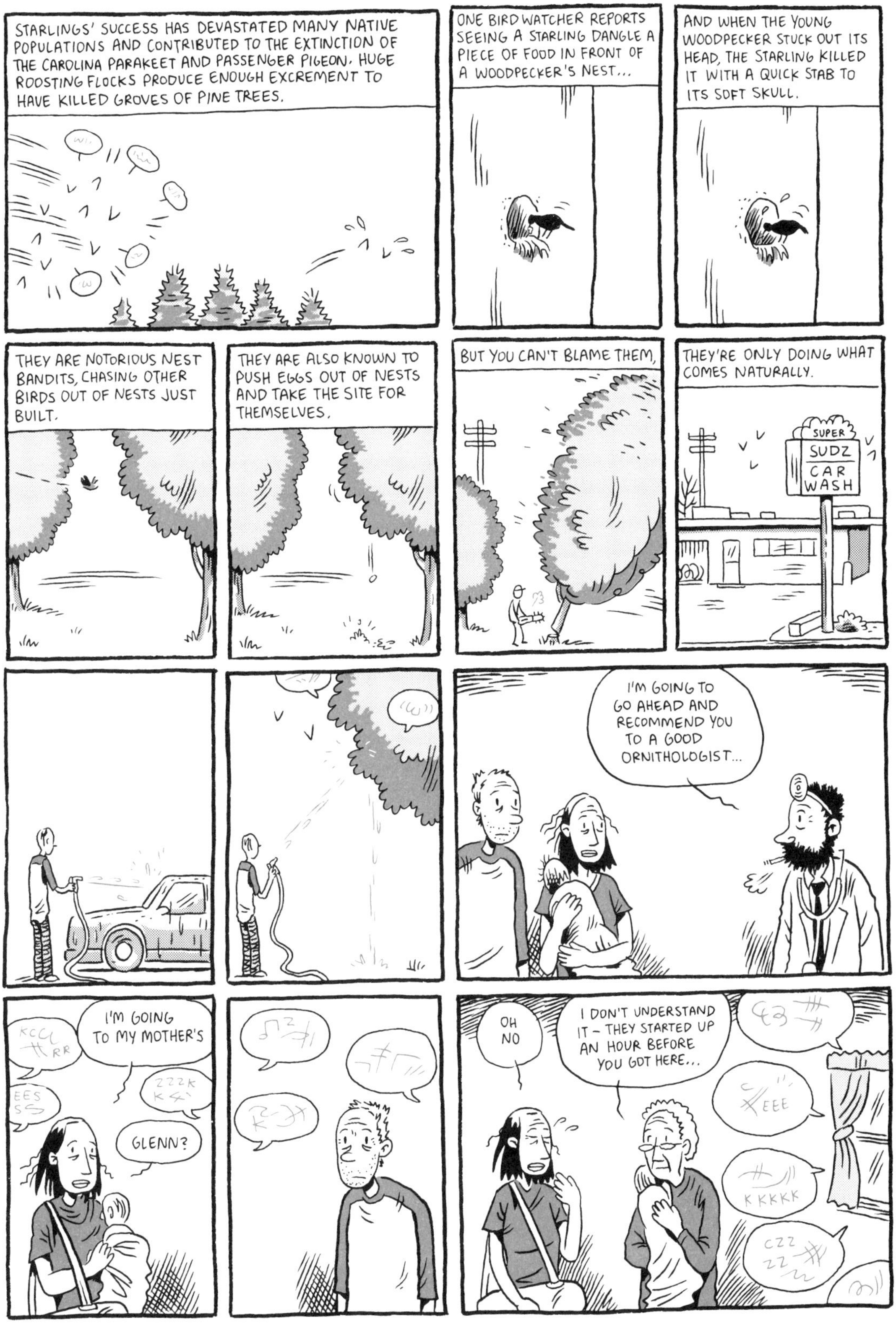
STARLINGS' SUCCESS HAS DEVASTATED MANY NATIVE POPULATIONS AND CONTRIBUTED TO THE EXTINCTION OF THE CAROLINA PARAKEET AND PASSENGER PIGEON. HUGE ROOSTING FLOCKS PRODUCE ENOUGH EXCREMENT TO HAVE KILLED GROVES OF PINE TREES.
ONE BIRD WATCHER REPORTS SEEING A STARLING DANGLE A PIECE OF FOOD IN FRONT OF A WOODPECKER'S NEST...
AND WHEN THE YOUNG WOODPECKER STUCK OUT ITS HEAD, THE STARLING KILLED IT WITH A QUICK STAB TO ITS SOFT SKULL.
THEY ARE NOTORIOUS NEST BANDITS, CHASING OTHER BIRDS OUT OF NESTS JUST BUILT.
THEY ARE ALSO KNOWN TO PUSH EGGS OUT OF NESTS AND TAKE THE SITE FOR THEMSELVES.
BUT YOU CAN'T BLAME THEM,
THEY'RE ONLY DOING WHAT COMES NATURALLY.
SUPER SUDZ CAR WASH
I'M GOING TO GO AHEAD AND RECOMMEND YOU TO A GOOD ORNITHOLOGIST...
I'M GOING TO MY MOTHER'S
GLENN?
OH NO
I DON'T UNDERSTAND IT - THEY STARTED UP AN HOUR BEFORE YOU GOT HERE...

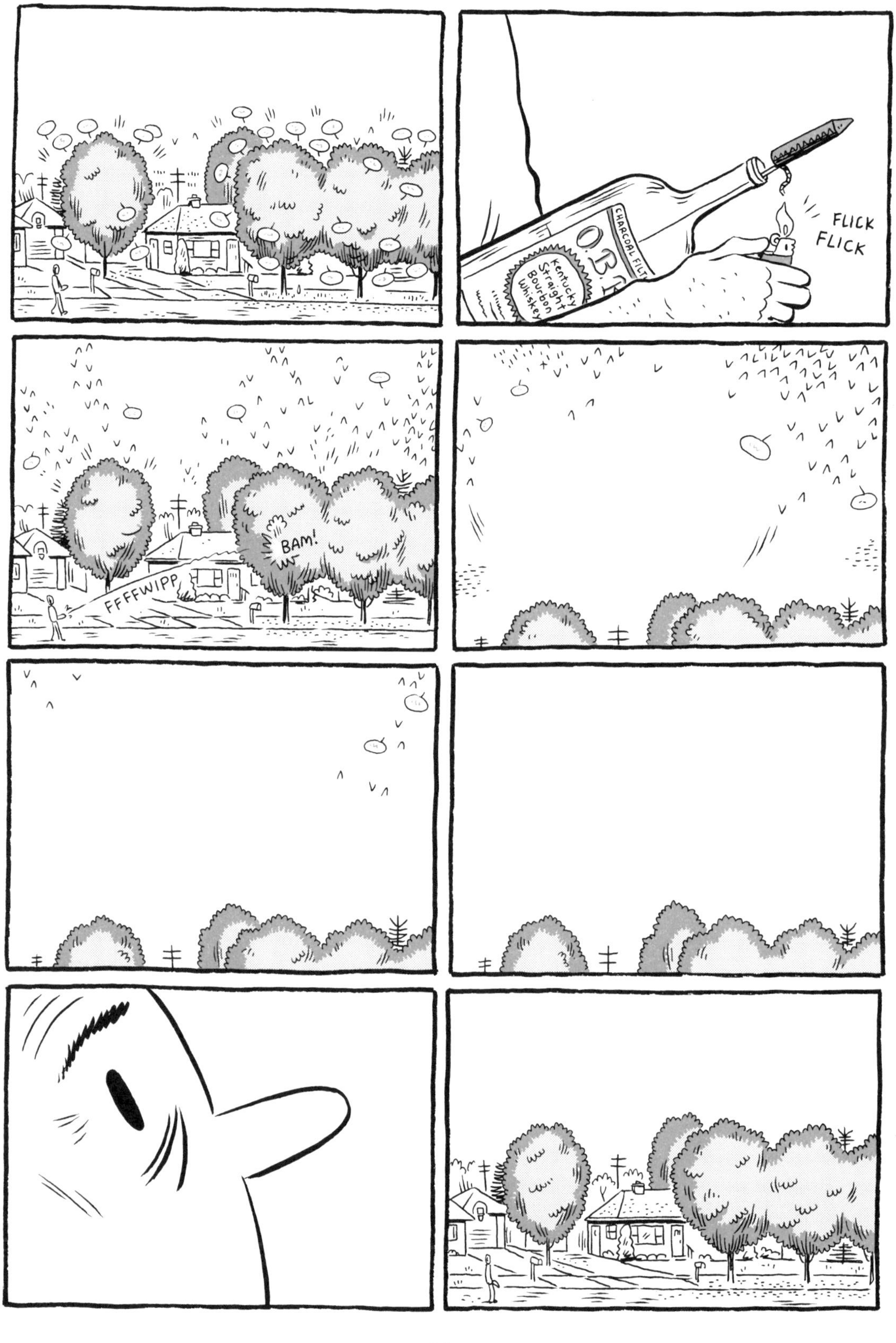
CHARCOAL FILT
O.B.
Kentucky
Straight
Bourbon
Whiskey
FLICK
FLICK
BAM!
FFFFWIPP

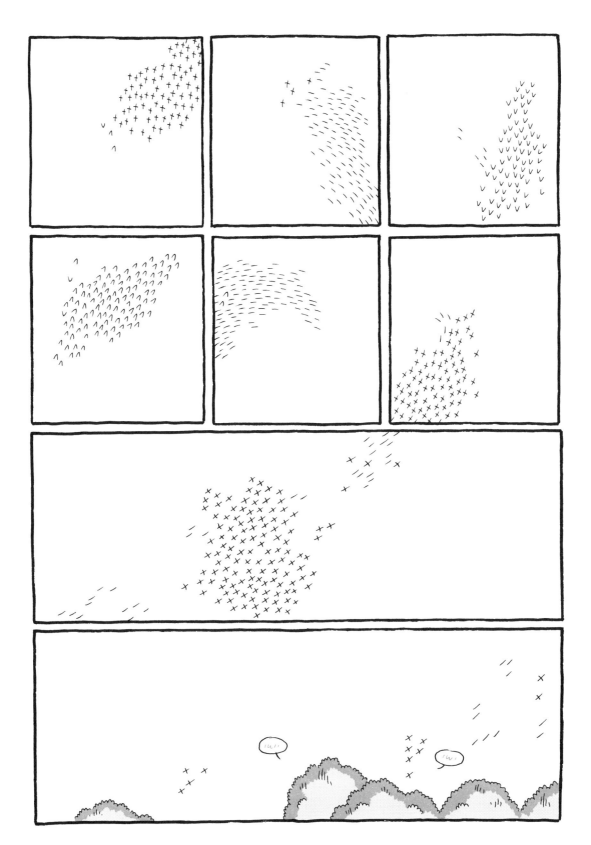

STARLINGS ARE NOT ONLY AGGRESSIVE, THEY ARE NOISY. BUT HIDDEN IN THE LOUD AND CONSTANT SQUAWKING, WHISTLING, CHIRPING, CLICKING AND BUZZING ARE MIMICKED SOUNDS—THE SONGS OF PARAKEETS, COWBIRDS, AND KILLDEER, AS WELL AS ENVIRONMENTAL SOUNDS— DOGS BARKING, CAR HORNS, CELL PHONES.

"AS MEMBERS OF THE *STURNIDAE* FAMILY, STARLINGS ARE COUSINS OF THE MYNAH BIRD AND ARE OUTSTANDING MIMICS," SAYS DAVID IAN WITHERS, ZOOLOGIST.

Mortimer

THE EARLIEST RECORD OF STARLING MIMICRY IS FROM ANCIENT ROME. PLINY THE ELDER MENTIONS HEARING ONE RECITE IN BOTH LATIN AND GREEK.

...et in terra pax

MOZART WAS SURPRISED TO OVERHEAR A CAGED STARLING WHISTLING ONE OF THE THEMES FROM THE FINAL MOVEMENT OF HIS OWN PIANO CONCERTO NO.17 IN G MAJOR, K.453.

HE BOUGHT THE BIRD AND KEPT IT AS A PET FOR SEVERAL YEARS.

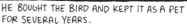

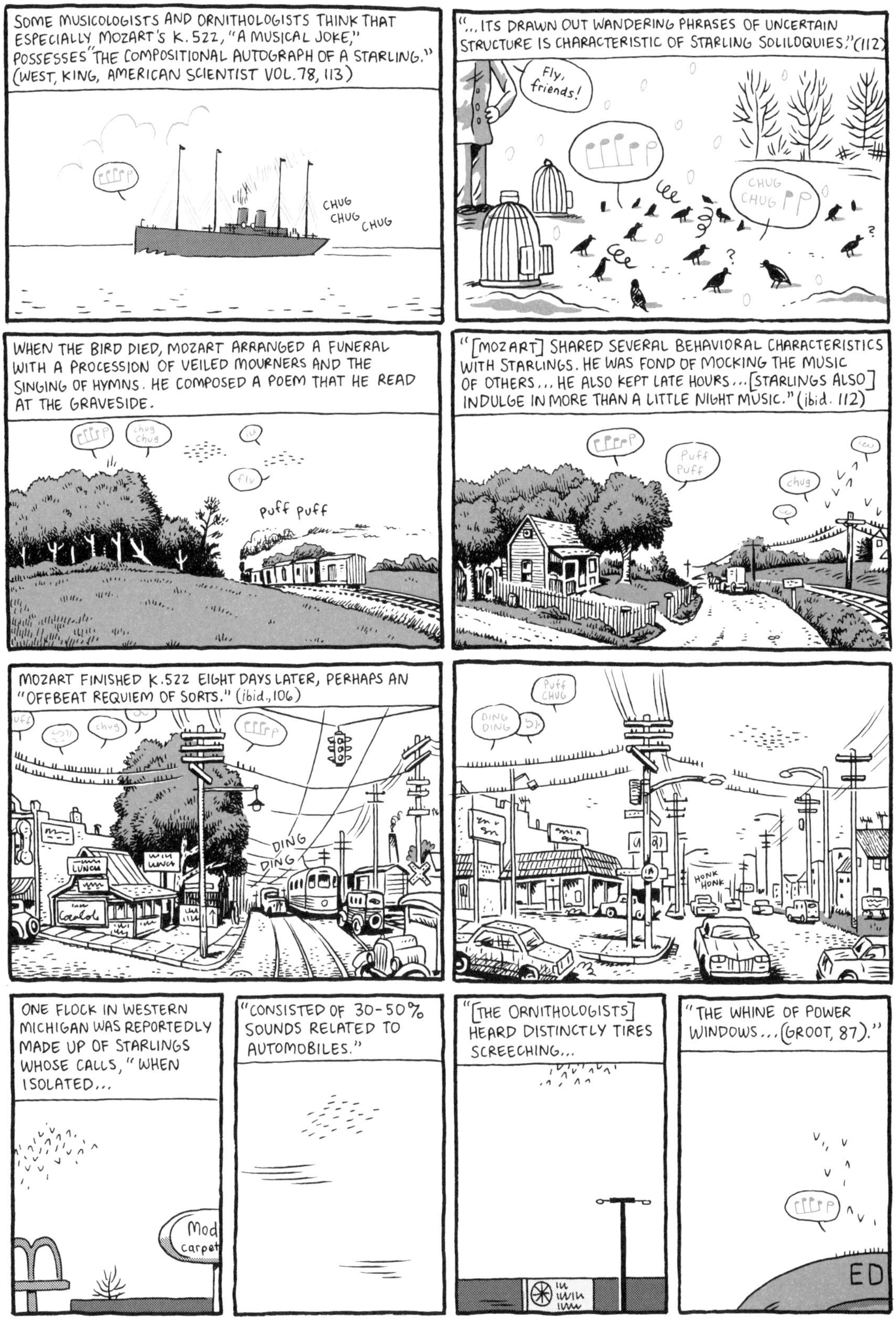
SOME MUSICOLOGISTS AND ORNITHOLOGISTS THINK THAT ESPECIALLY MOZART'S K. 522, "A MUSICAL JOKE," POSSESSES "THE COMPOSITIONAL AUTOGRAPH OF A STARLING." (WEST, KING, AMERICAN SCIENTIST VOL. 78, 113)
CHUG CHUG CHUG
"...ITS DRAWN OUT WANDERING PHRASES OF UNCERTAIN STRUCTURE IS CHARACTERISTIC OF STARLING SOLILOQUIES." (112)
Fly, friends!
CHUG CHUG
WHEN THE BIRD DIED, MOZART ARRANGED A FUNERAL WITH A PROCESSION OF VEILED MOURNERS AND THE SINGING OF HYMNS. HE COMPOSED A POEM THAT HE READ AT THE GRAVESIDE.
chug chug
fly
puff puff
"[MOZART] SHARED SEVERAL BEHAVIORAL CHARACTERISTICS WITH STARLINGS. HE WAS FOND OF MOCKING THE MUSIC OF OTHERS... HE ALSO KEPT LATE HOURS... [STARLINGS ALSO] INDULGE IN MORE THAN A LITTLE NIGHT MUSIC." (ibid. 112)
Puff Puff
chug
MOZART FINISHED K. 522 EIGHT DAYS LATER, PERHAPS AN "OFFBEAT REQUIEM OF SORTS." (ibid., 106)
chug
LUNCH
DING DING
Puff CHUG
DING DING
HONK HONK
ONE FLOCK IN WESTERN MICHIGAN WAS REPORTEDLY MADE UP OF STARLINGS WHOSE CALLS, "WHEN ISOLATED...
Mod carpet
"CONSISTED OF 30-50% SOUNDS RELATED TO AUTOMOBILES."
"[THE ORNITHOLOGISTS] HEARD DISTINCTLY TIRES SCREECHING...
"THE WHINE OF POWER WINDOWS... (GROOT, 87)."
ED

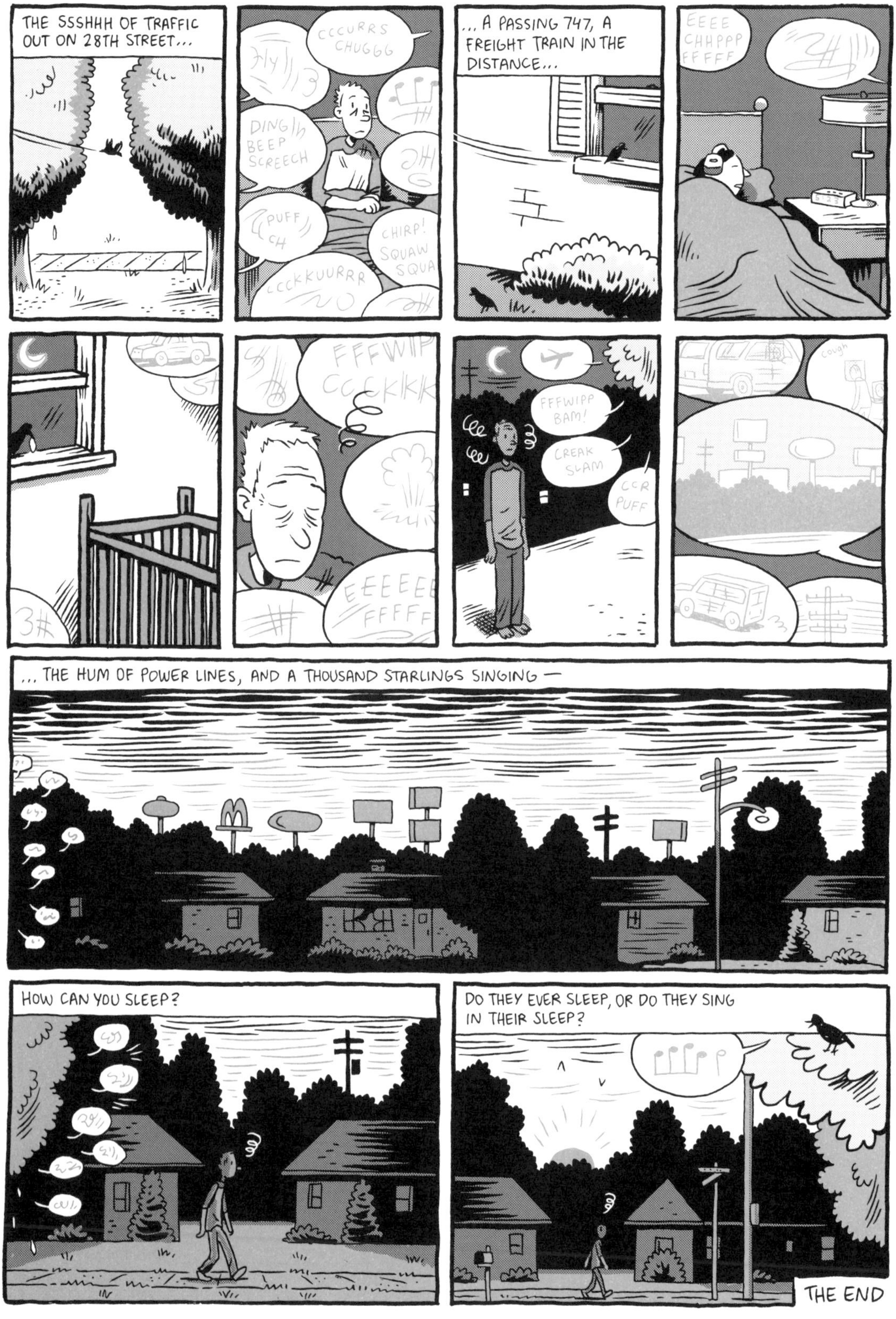

THE SSSHHH OF TRAFFIC OUT ON 28TH STREET...
CCCURRS CHUGGG
DING
BEEP
SCREECH
PUFF CH
CHIRP! SQUAW SQUA
CCCKKUURRR
... A PASSING 747, A FREIGHT TRAIN IN THE DISTANCE...
EEEE CHHPPP FFFFF
FFFWIP CCCKIKK
EEEEEE FFFFF
FFFWIPP BAM!
CREAK SLAM
CCR PUFF
cough
... THE HUM OF POWER LINES, AND A THOUSAND STARLINGS SINGING —
HOW CAN YOU SLEEP?
DO THEY EVER SLEEP, OR DO THEY SING IN THEIR SLEEP?
THE END

Nicolas Robel

Nicolas Robel was born in Quebec City, Canada in 1974. By age four he moved with his family to Switzerland and he currently makes his home in Geneva, where he is a designer for his own graphic arts firm, B.ü.L.b Grafix. Through his company Robel has published a number of European and American cartoonists in a variety of silk-screened booklets that are often created in unique and unusual formats. One of these is a series of two inch by four inch boxes that effectively redefines the term "mini-comics"; they each contain a comic strip folded over several times until they are small enough to fit into their tiny compartments.

Robel is currently working on two new stories, MAN OF STEEL and LOVE AND DISASTER, both of which will be published by next year. A newcomer to North American comics, Robel's first story in English was published in DRAWN & QUARTERLY VOLUME 4 in 2001.

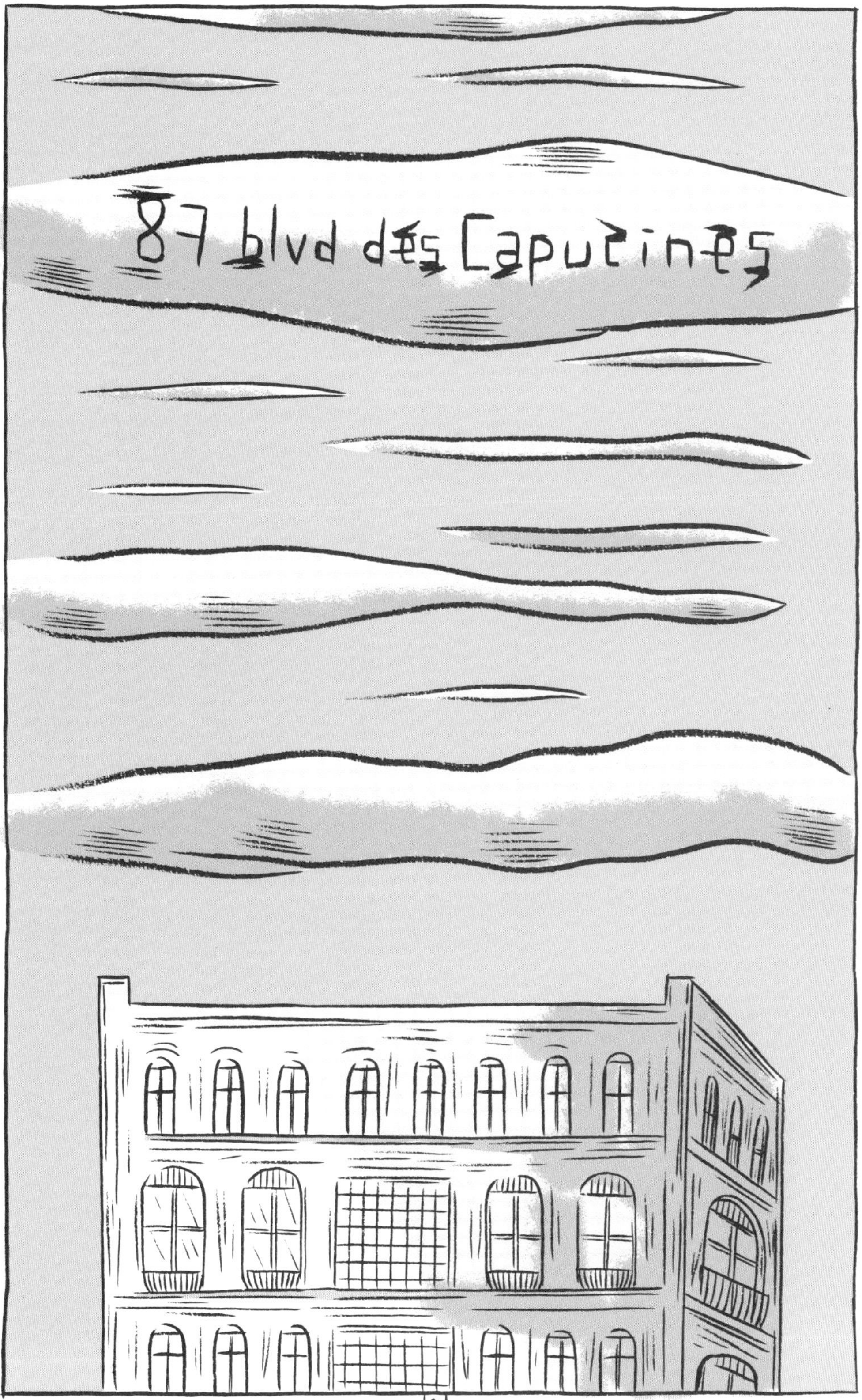
87 blvd des Capucines

1

TRANSLATED BY HELGE DASCHER.

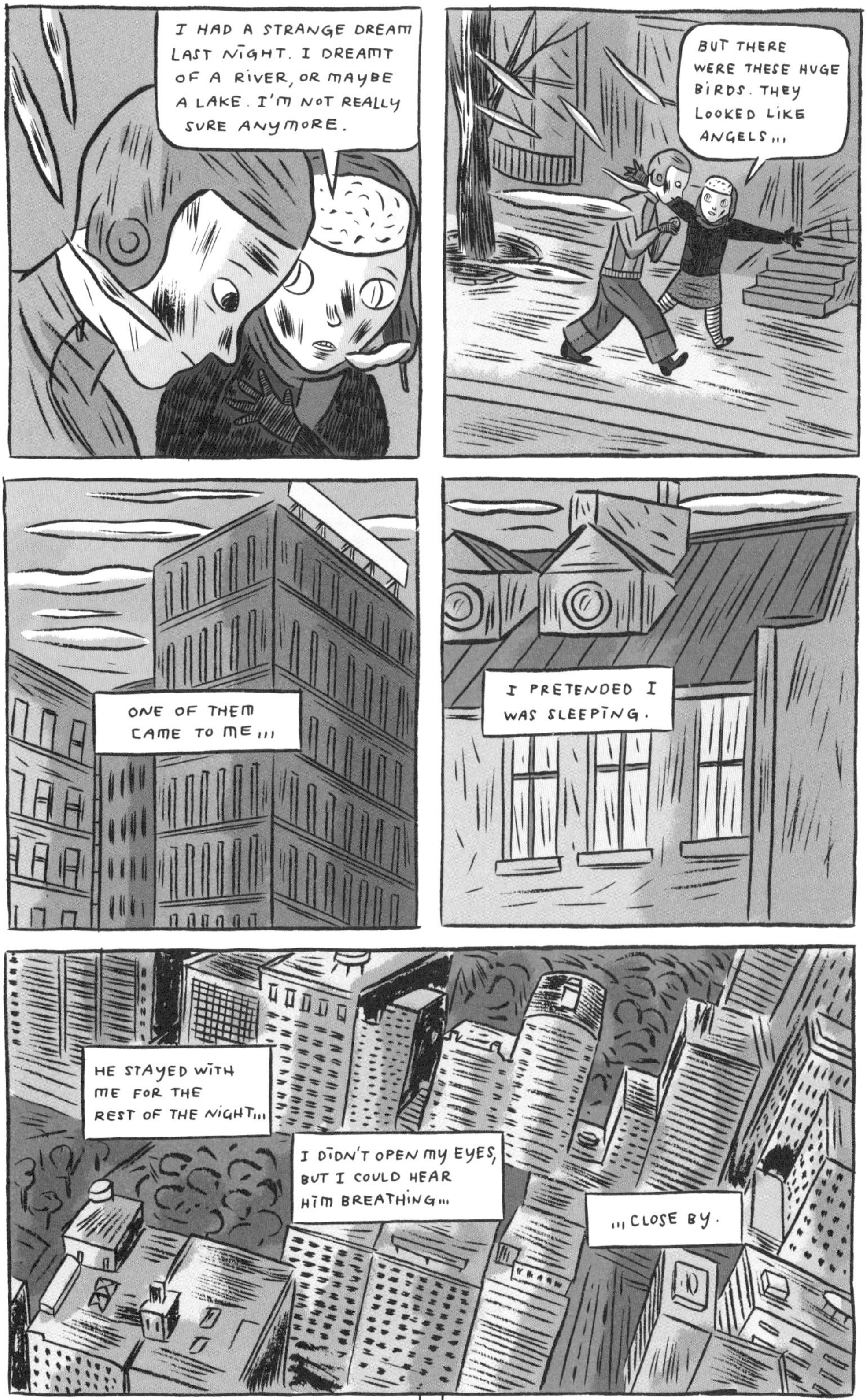
I HAD A STRANGE DREAM LAST NIGHT. I DREAMT OF A RIVER, OR MAYBE A LAKE. I'M NOT REALLY SURE ANYMORE.
BUT THERE WERE THESE HUGE BIRDS. THEY LOOKED LIKE ANGELS...
ONE OF THEM CAME TO ME...
I PRETENDED I WAS SLEEPING.
HE STAYED WITH ME FOR THE REST OF THE NIGHT...
I DIDN'T OPEN MY EYES, BUT I COULD HEAR HIM BREATHING...
...CLOSE BY.

3

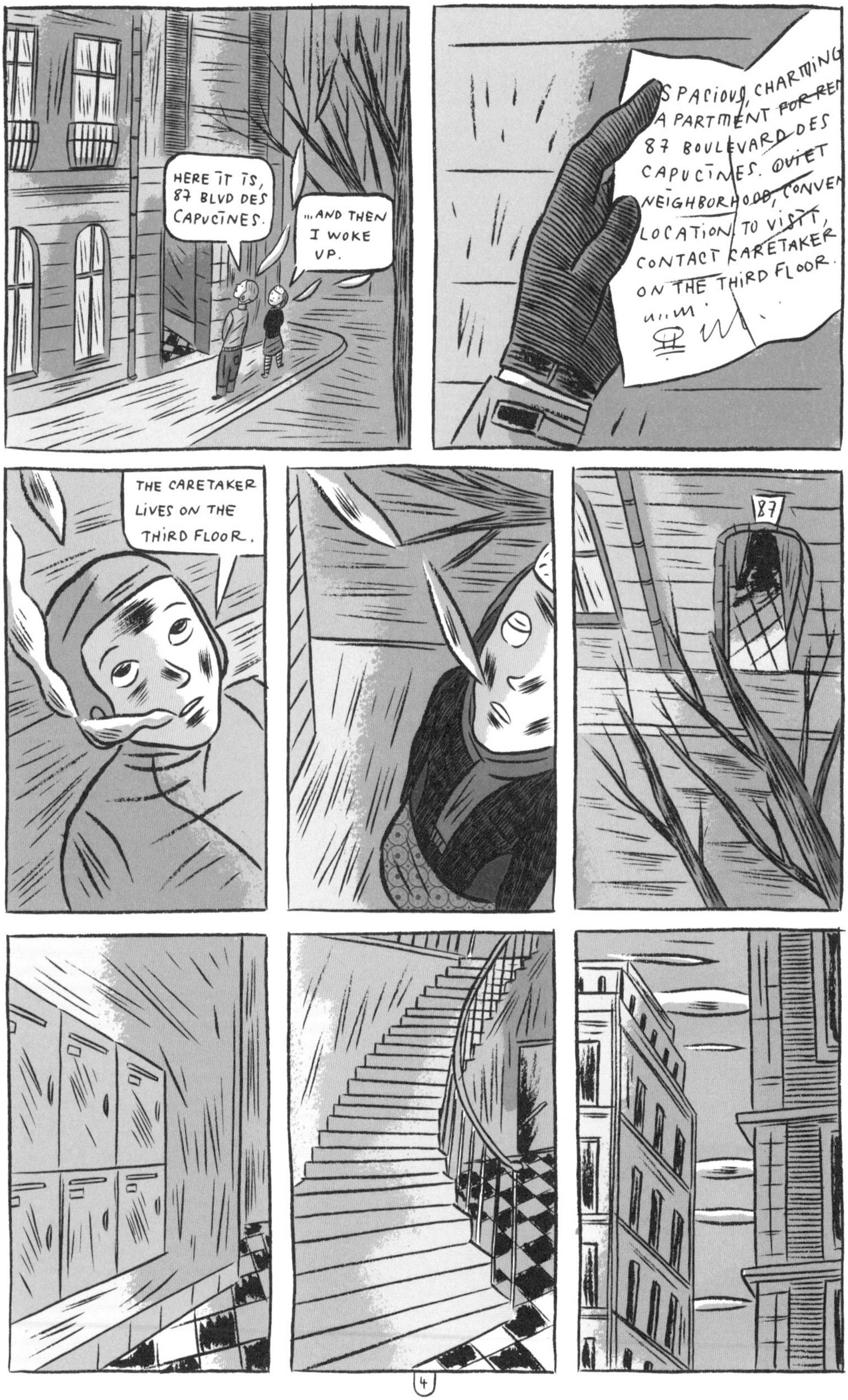
HERE IT IS, 87 BLVD DES CAPUCINES.
...AND THEN I WOKE UP.
SPACIOUS, CHARMING APARTMENT FOR REN 87 BOULEVARD DES CAPUCINES. QUIET NEIGHBORHOOD, CONVEN LOCATION. TO VISIT, CONTACT CARETAKER ON THE THIRD FLOOR.
THE CARETAKER LIVES ON THE THIRD FLOOR.
87

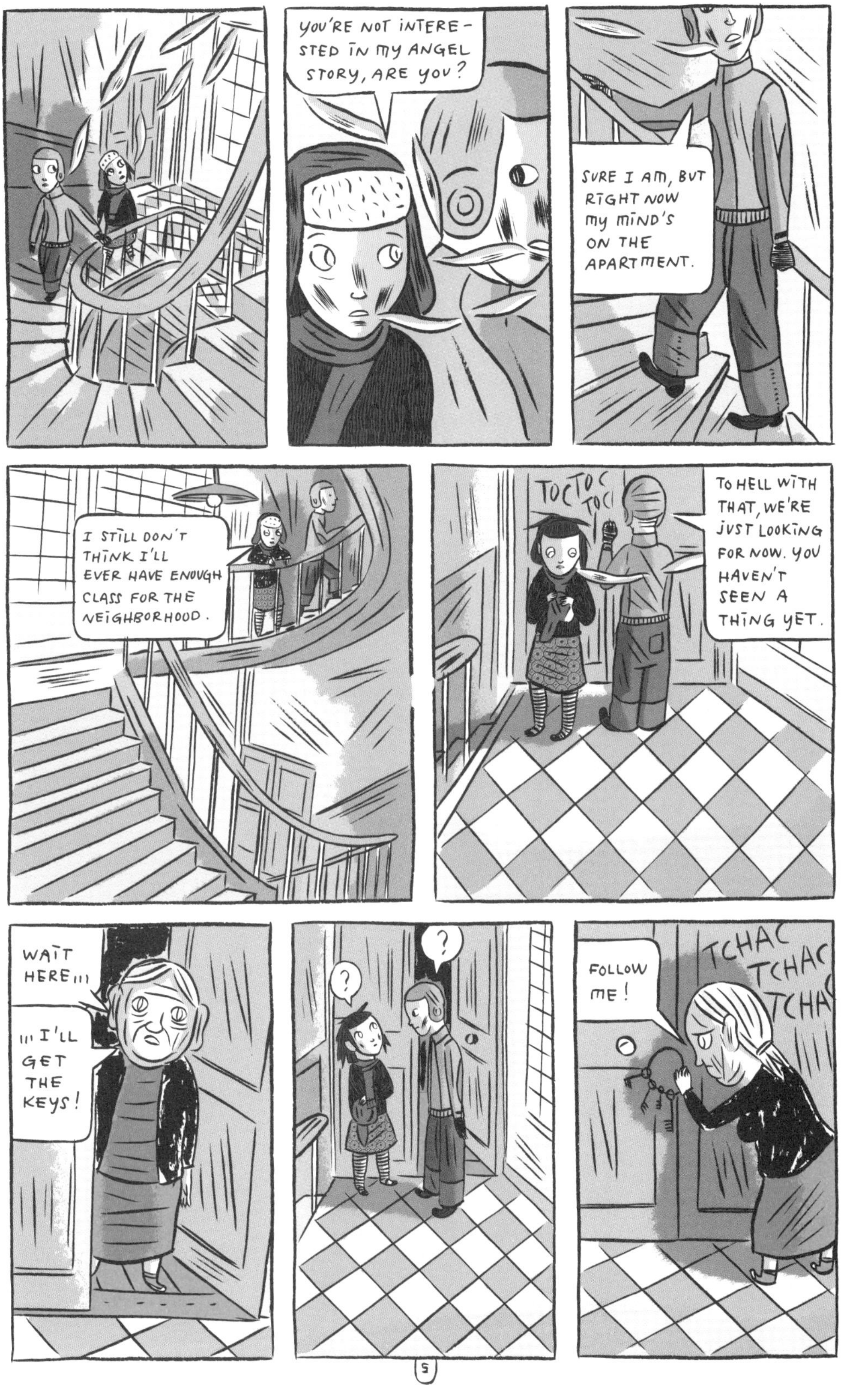

YOU'RE NOT INTERESTED IN MY ANGEL STORY, ARE YOU?
SURE I AM, BUT RIGHT NOW MY MIND'S ON THE APARTMENT.
I STILL DON'T THINK I'LL EVER HAVE ENOUGH CLASS FOR THE NEIGHBORHOOD.
TOC TOC TOC
TO HELL WITH THAT, WE'RE JUST LOOKING FOR NOW. YOU HAVEN'T SEEN A THING YET.
WAIT HERE...
...I'LL GET THE KEYS!
?
?
FOLLOW ME!
TCHAC TCHAC TCHAC

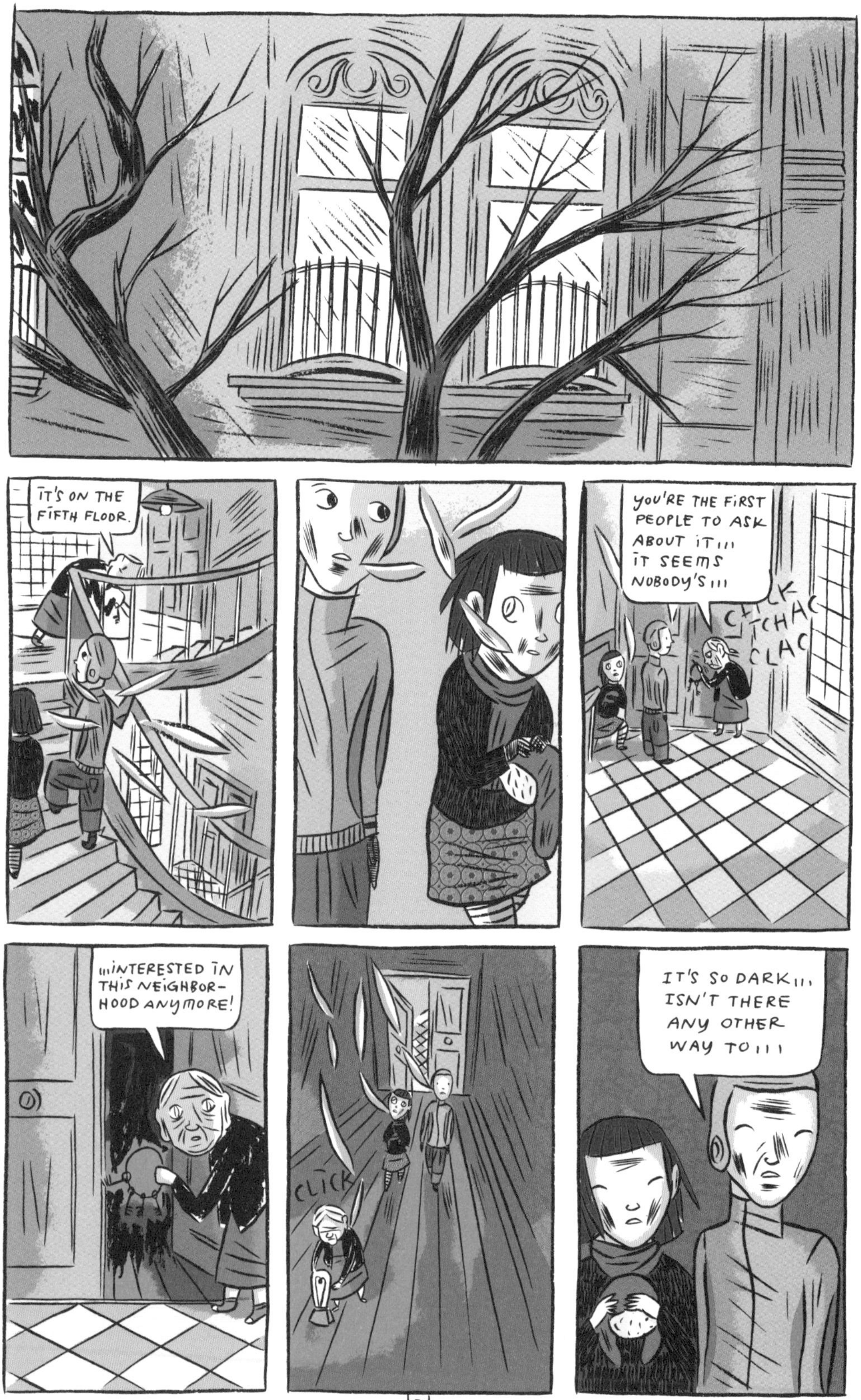
IT'S ON THE FIFTH FLOOR.
YOU'RE THE FIRST PEOPLE TO ASK ABOUT IT... IT SEEMS NOBODY'S...
CLICK CHAC CLAC
...INTERESTED IN THIS NEIGHBOR-HOOD ANYMORE!
CLICK
IT'S SO DARK... ISN'T THERE ANY OTHER WAY TO...
6

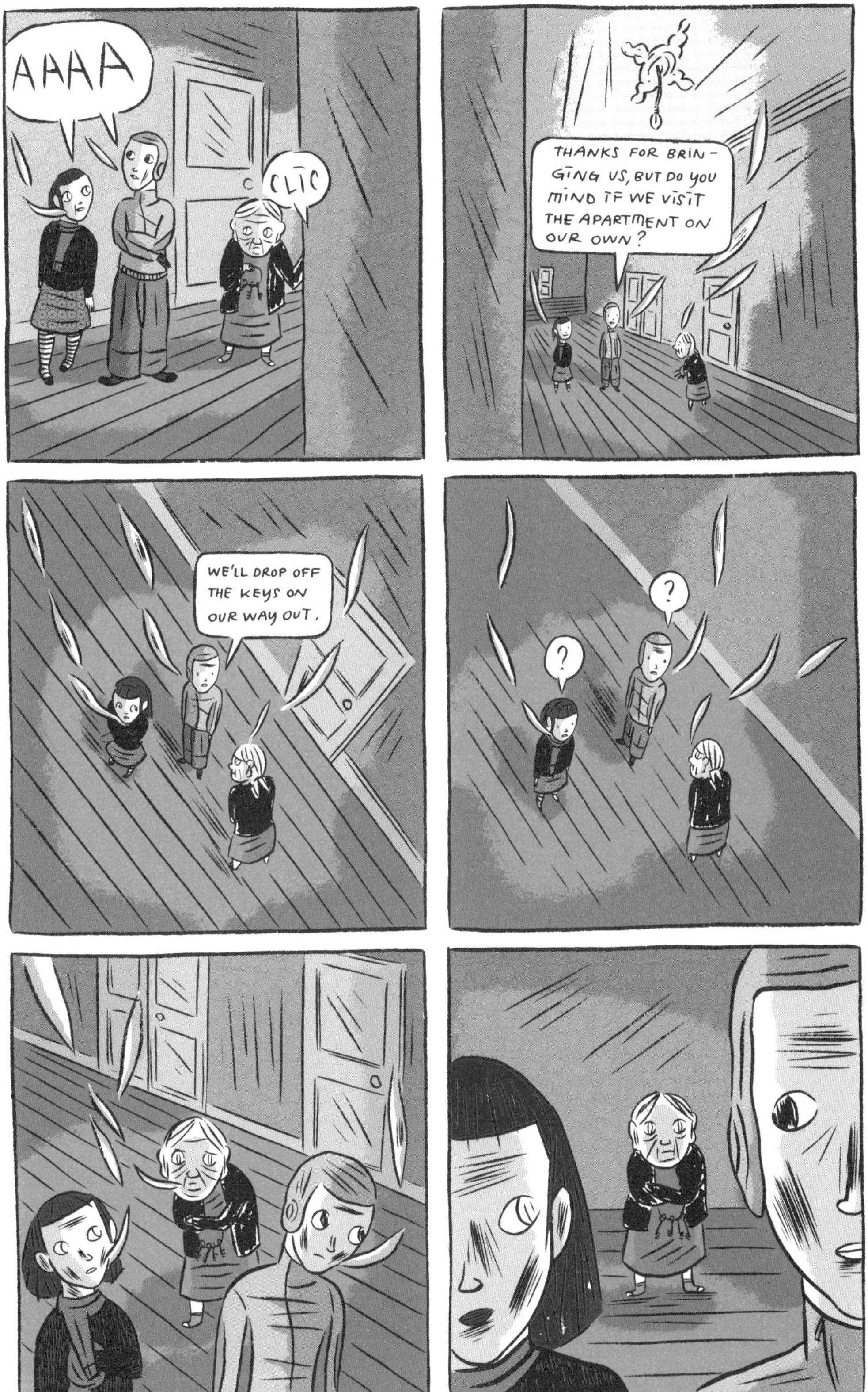
AAAA
CLIC
THANKS FOR BRINGING US, BUT DO YOU MIND IF WE VISIT THE APARTMENT ON OUR OWN?
WE'LL DROP OFF THE KEYS ON OUR WAY OUT.
?
?
7

?
HA
HA
HA
HA, HA
SHUSH!
CLICK
HA HAHA

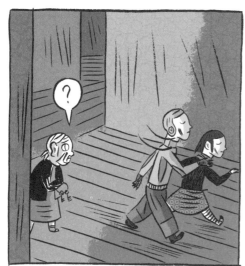

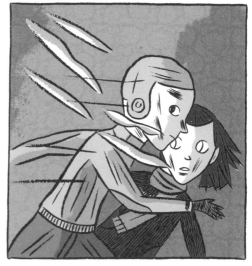

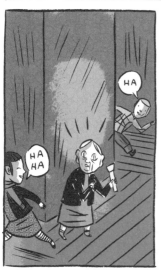

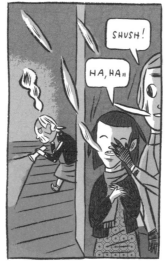

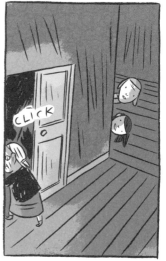

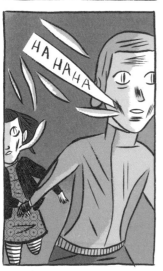

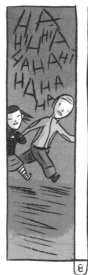

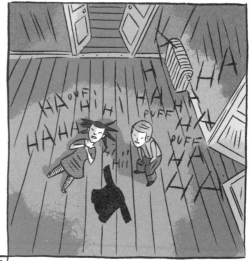

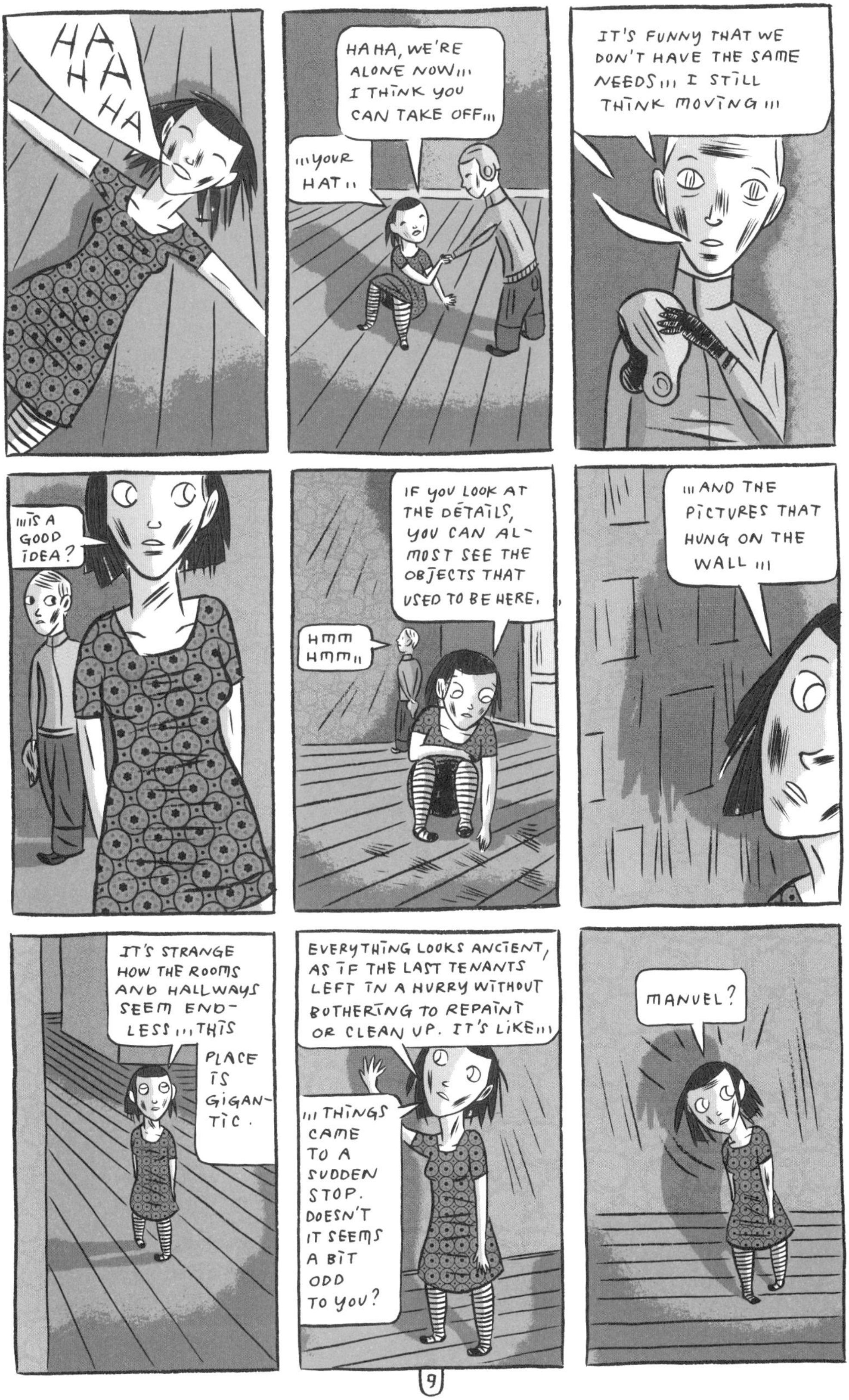
HA HA HA HA
HA HA, WE'RE ALONE NOW... I THINK YOU CAN TAKE OFF...
...YOUR HAT..
IT'S FUNNY THAT WE DON'T HAVE THE SAME NEEDS... I STILL THINK MOVING...
...IS A GOOD IDEA?
IF YOU LOOK AT THE DETAILS, YOU CAN ALMOST SEE THE OBJECTS THAT USED TO BE HERE.
HMM HMM..
...AND THE PICTURES THAT HUNG ON THE WALL...
IT'S STRANGE HOW THE ROOMS AND HALLWAYS SEEM ENDLESS... THIS PLACE IS GIGANTIC.
EVERYTHING LOOKS ANCIENT, AS IF THE LAST TENANTS LEFT IN A HURRY WITHOUT BOTHERING TO REPAINT OR CLEAN UP. IT'S LIKE...
...THINGS CAME TO A SUDDEN STOP. DOESN'T IT SEEMS A BIT ODD TO YOU?
MANUEL?
9

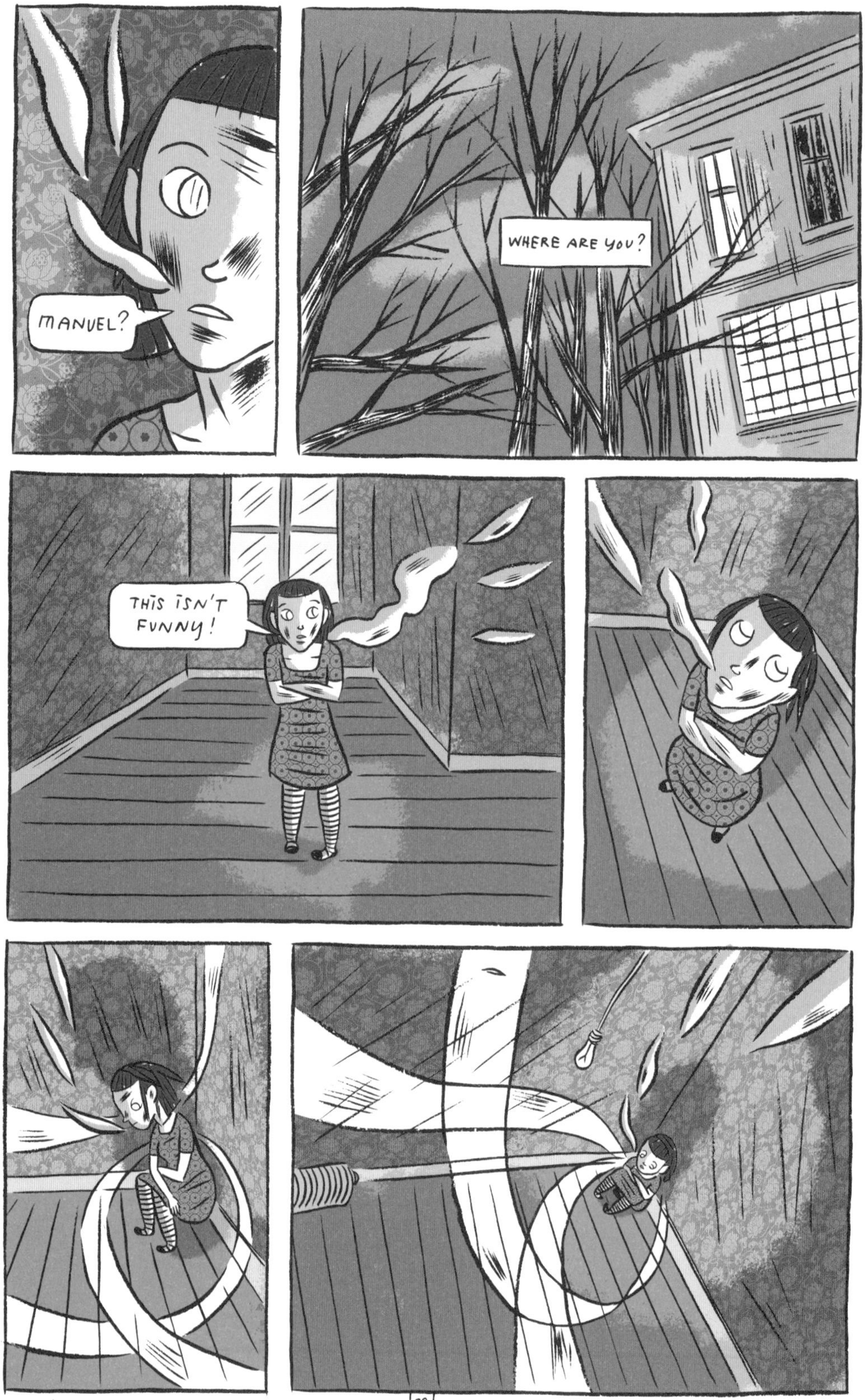
MANUEL?
WHERE ARE YOU?
THIS ISN'T FUNNY!
10

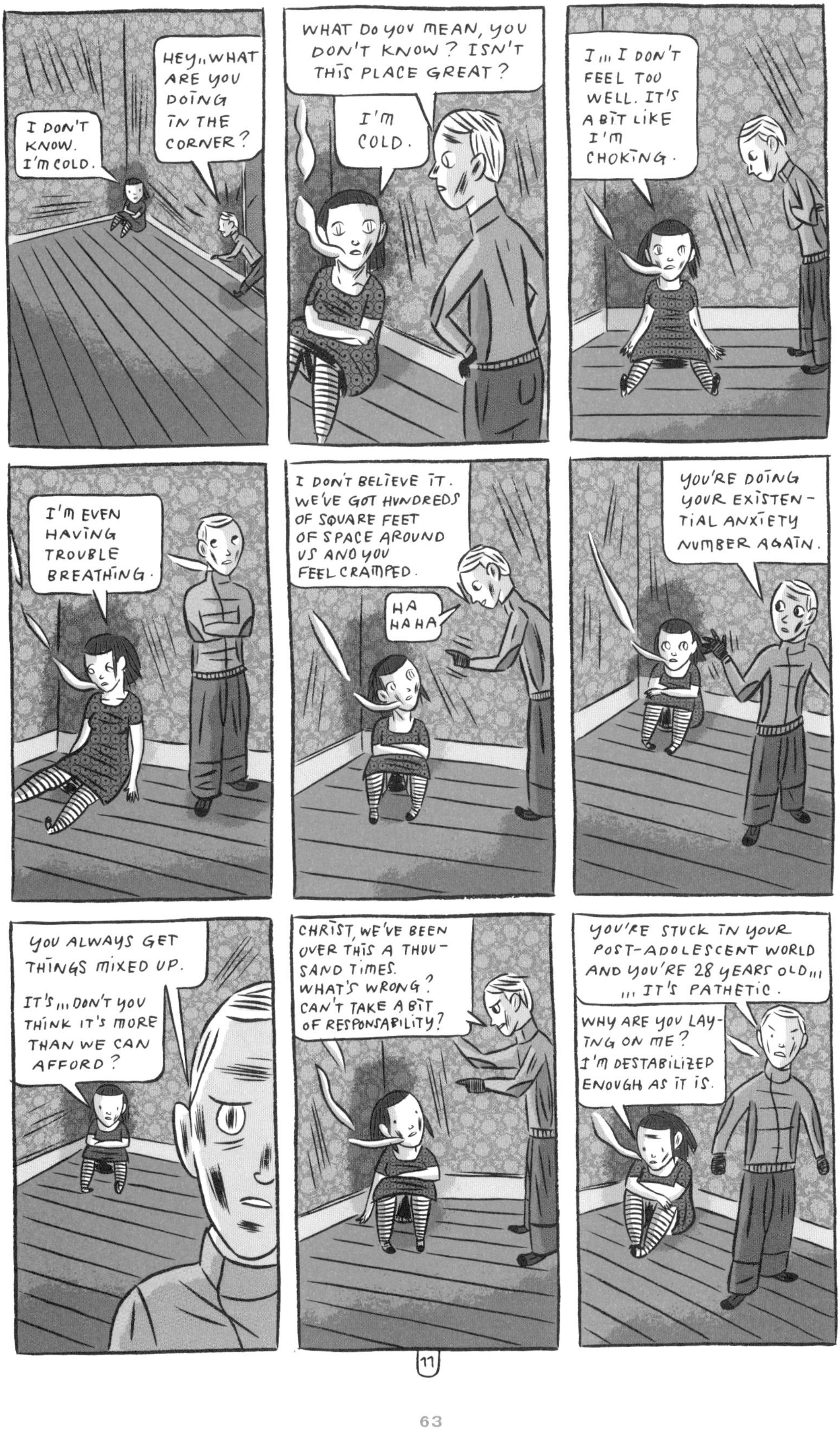
HEY,, WHAT ARE YOU DOING IN THE CORNER?
I DON'T KNOW. I'M COLD.
WHAT DO YOU MEAN, YOU DON'T KNOW? ISN'T THIS PLACE GREAT?
I'M COLD.
I,,, I DON'T FEEL TOO WELL. IT'S A BIT LIKE I'M CHOKING.
I'M EVEN HAVING TROUBLE BREATHING.
I DON'T BELIEVE IT. WE'VE GOT HUNDREDS OF SQUARE FEET OF SPACE AROUND US AND YOU FEEL CRAMPED.
HA HA HA
YOU'RE DOING YOUR EXISTEN-TIAL ANXIETY NUMBER AGAIN.
YOU ALWAYS GET THINGS MIXED UP.
IT'S,,, DON'T YOU THINK IT'S MORE THAN WE CAN AFFORD?
CHRIST, WE'VE BEEN OVER THIS A THOU-SAND TIMES. WHAT'S WRONG? CAN'T TAKE A BIT OF RESPONSABILITY?
YOU'RE STUCK IN YOUR POST-ADOLESCENT WORLD AND YOU'RE 28 YEARS OLD,,, ,,, IT'S PATHETIC.
WHY ARE YOU LAY-ING ON ME? I'M DESTABILIZED ENOUGH AS IT IS.
11

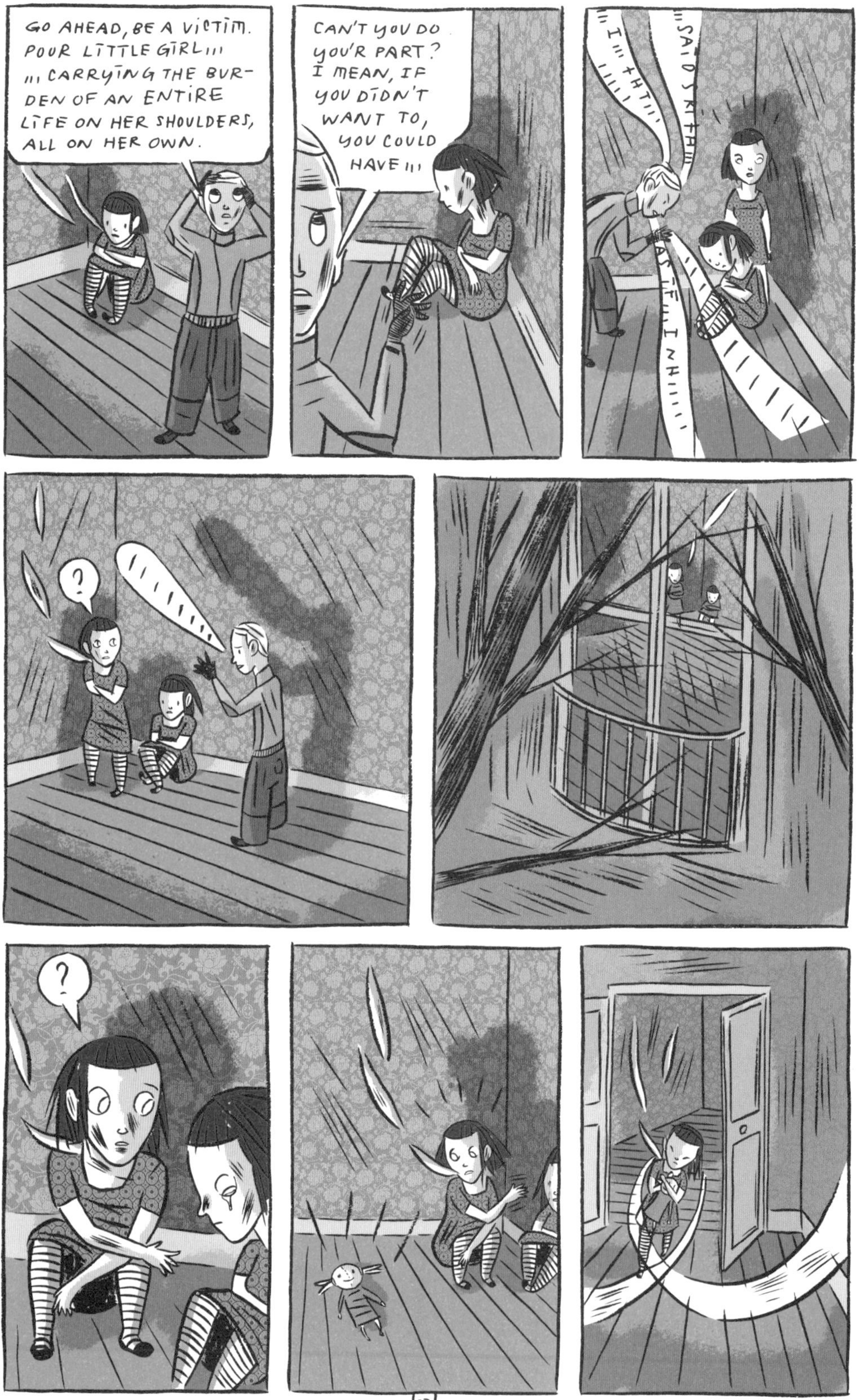
GO AHEAD, BE A VICTIM. POUR LITTLE GIRL... ...CARRYING THE BURDEN OF AN ENTIRE LIFE ON HER SHOULDERS, ALL ON HER OWN.
CAN'T YOU DO YOU'R PART? I MEAN, IF YOU DIDN'T WANT TO, YOU COULD HAVE...
?
?

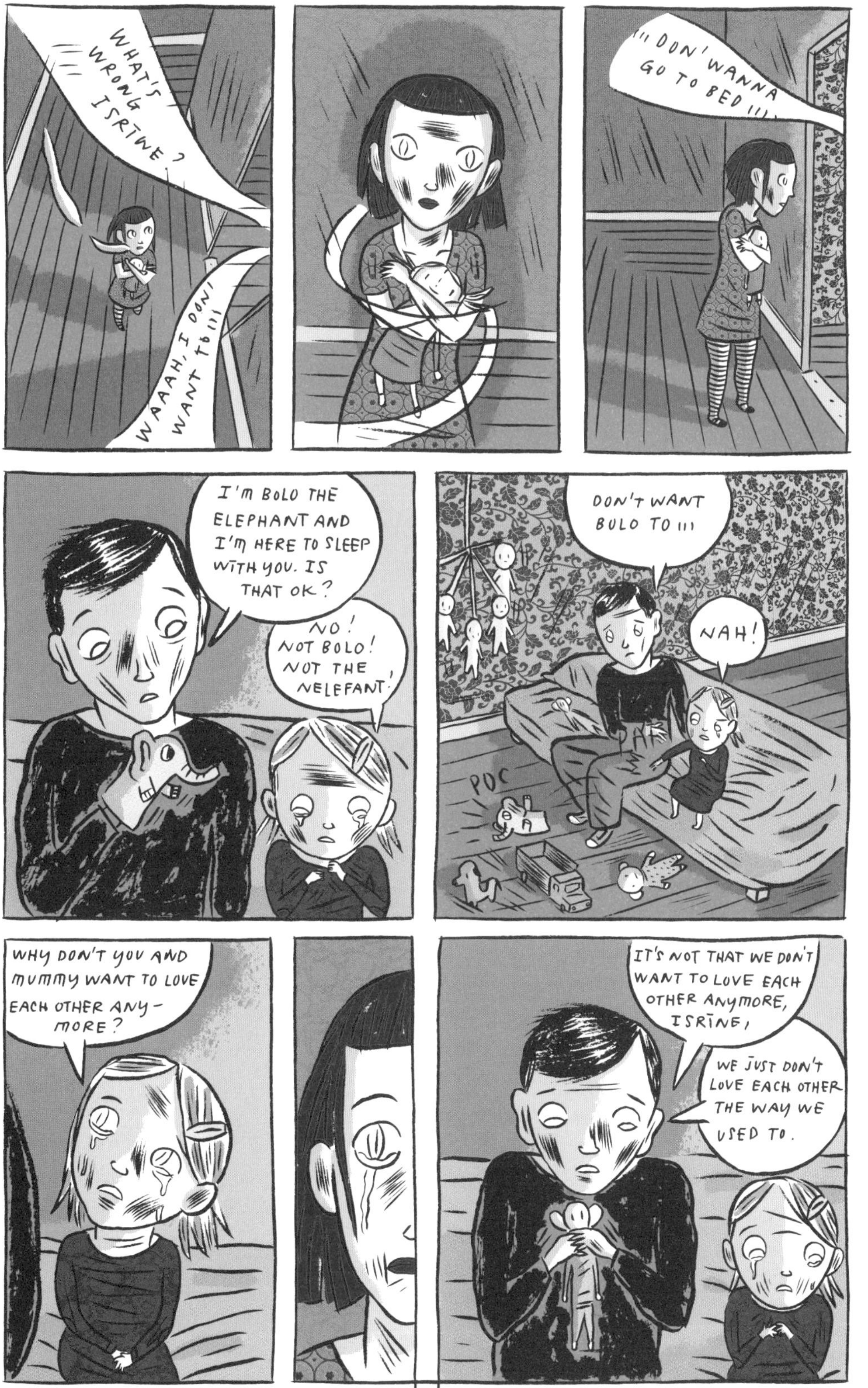
WHAT'S WRONG ISRĪNE?
WAAAH, I DON'T WANT TO!!!
!!! DON' WANNA GO TO BED!!!
I'M BOLO THE ELEPHANT AND I'M HERE TO SLEEP WITH YOU. IS THAT OK?
NO! NOT BOLO! NOT THE NELEFANT!
DON'T WANT BOLO TO!!!
NAH!
PAF
POC
WHY DON'T YOU AND MUMMY WANT TO LOVE EACH OTHER ANY-MORE?
IT'S NOT THAT WE DON'T WANT TO LOVE EACH OTHER ANYMORE, ISRĪNE,
WE JUST DON'T LOVE EACH OTHER THE WAY WE USED TO.
73

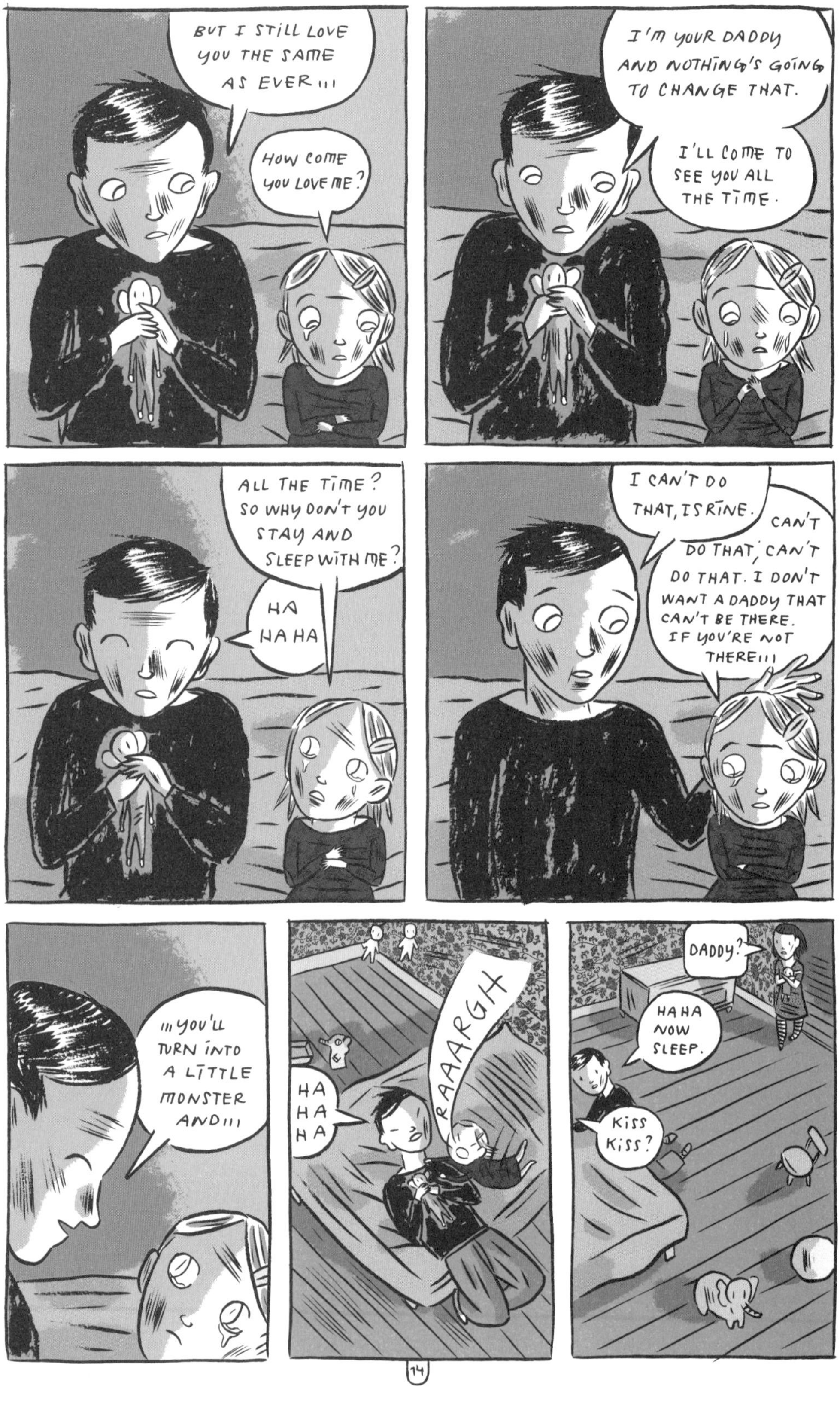

BUT I STILL LOVE YOU THE SAME AS EVER...
HOW COME YOU LOVE ME?
I'M YOUR DADDY AND NOTHING'S GOING TO CHANGE THAT.
I'LL COME TO SEE YOU ALL THE TIME.
ALL THE TIME? SO WHY DON'T YOU STAY AND SLEEP WITH ME?
HA HA HA
I CAN'T DO THAT, ISRINE.
CAN'T DO THAT, CAN'T DO THAT. I DON'T WANT A DADDY THAT CAN'T BE THERE. IF YOU'RE NOT THERE...
...YOU'LL TURN INTO A LITTLE MONSTER AND...
RAAARGH
HA HA HA
DADDY?
HA HA NOW SLEEP.
KISS KISS?
74

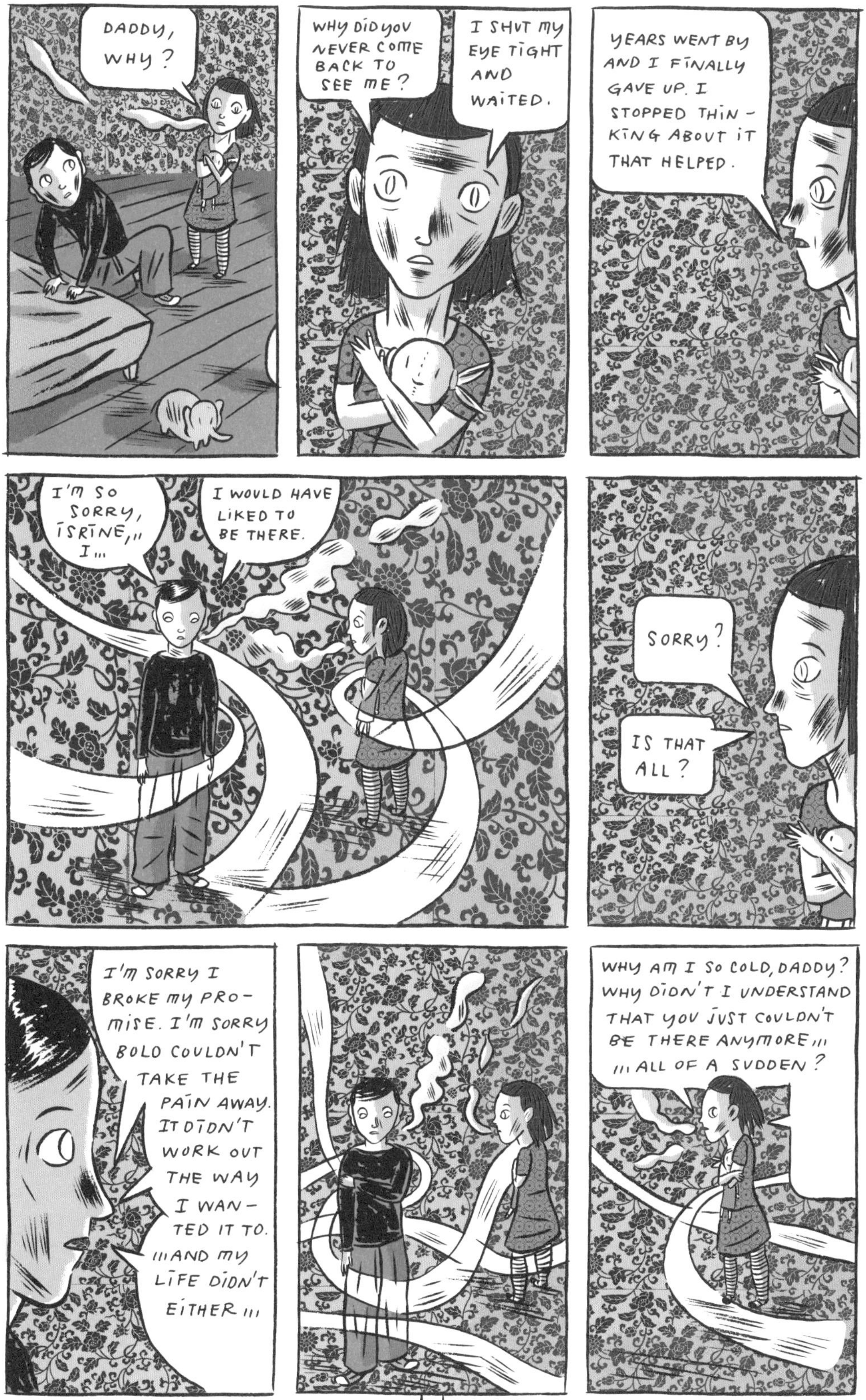
DADDY, WHY?
WHY DID YOU NEVER COME BACK TO SEE ME?
I SHUT MY EYE TIGHT AND WAITED.
YEARS WENT BY AND I FINALLY GAVE UP. I STOPPED THIN-KING ABOUT IT THAT HELPED.
I'M SO SORRY, ISRINE,,, I,,,
I WOULD HAVE LIKED TO BE THERE.
SORRY?
IS THAT ALL?
I'M SORRY I BROKE MY PRO-MISE. I'M SORRY BOLO COULDN'T TAKE THE PAIN AWAY. IT DIDN'T WORK OUT THE WAY I WAN-TED IT TO.
,,,AND MY LIFE DIDN'T EITHER,,,
WHY AM I SO COLD, DADDY? WHY DIDN'T I UNDERSTAND THAT YOU JUST COULDN'T BE THERE ANYMORE,,,
,,, ALL OF A SUDDEN?
15

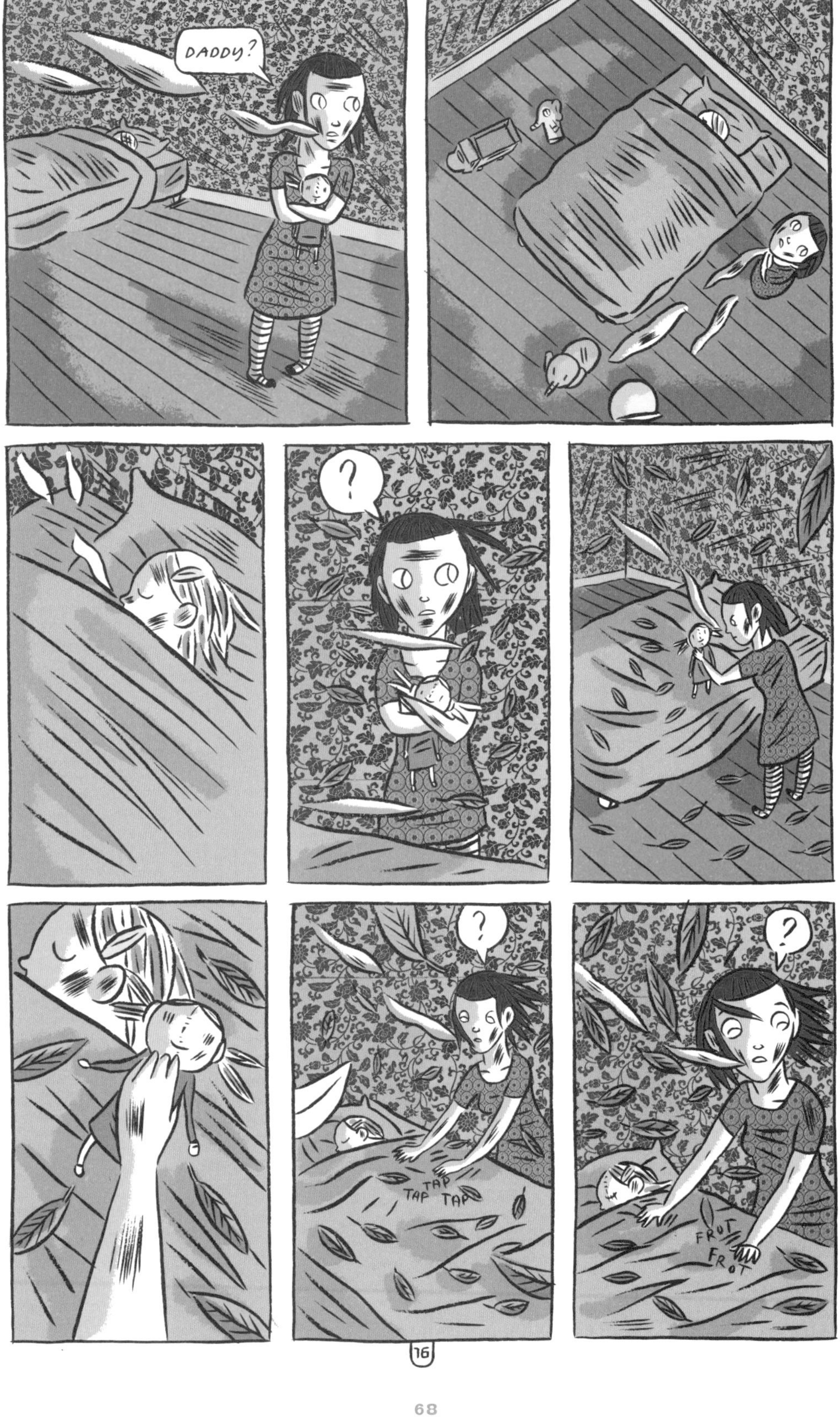
DADDY?
?
TAP
TAP TAP TAP
?
?
FROT
FROT

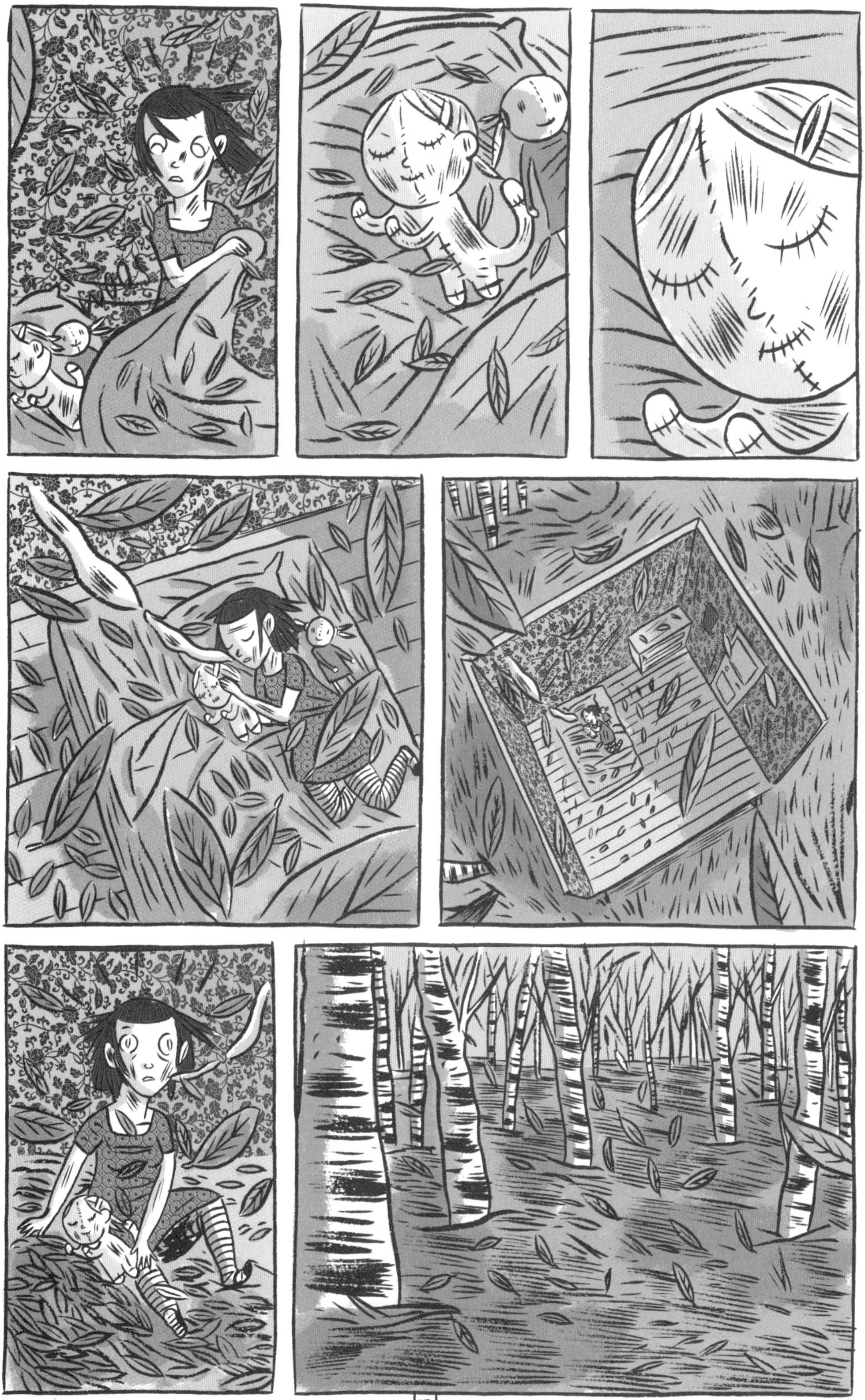

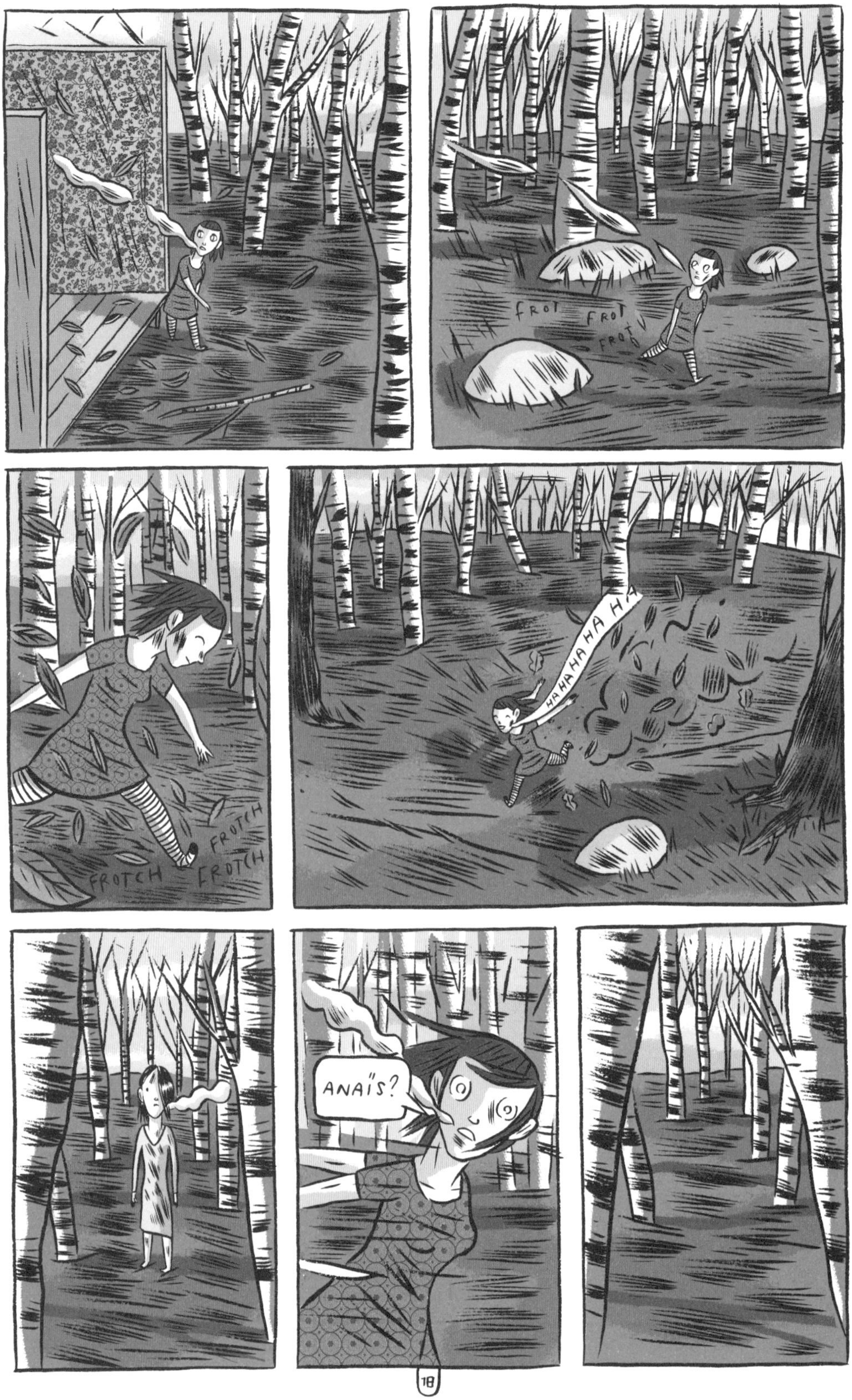
FROT
FROT
FROT
FROTCH
FROTCH
FROTCH
HA HA HA HA HA
ANAÏS?
18

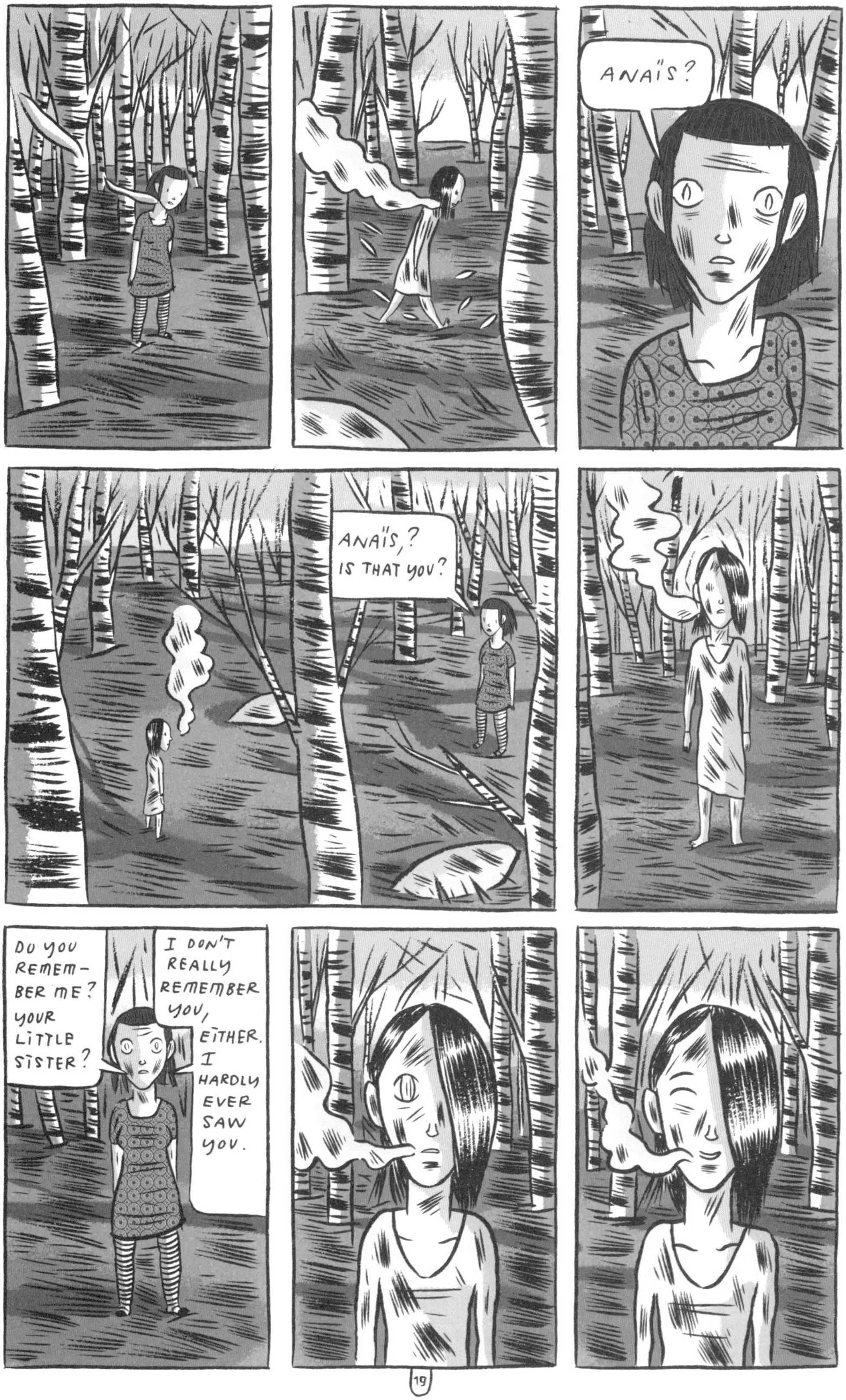

ANAÏS?
ANAÏS,?
IS THAT YOU?
DO YOU REMEM-BER ME? YOUR LITTLE SISTER?
I DON'T REALLY REMEMBER YOU, EITHER. I HARDLY EVER SAW YOU.

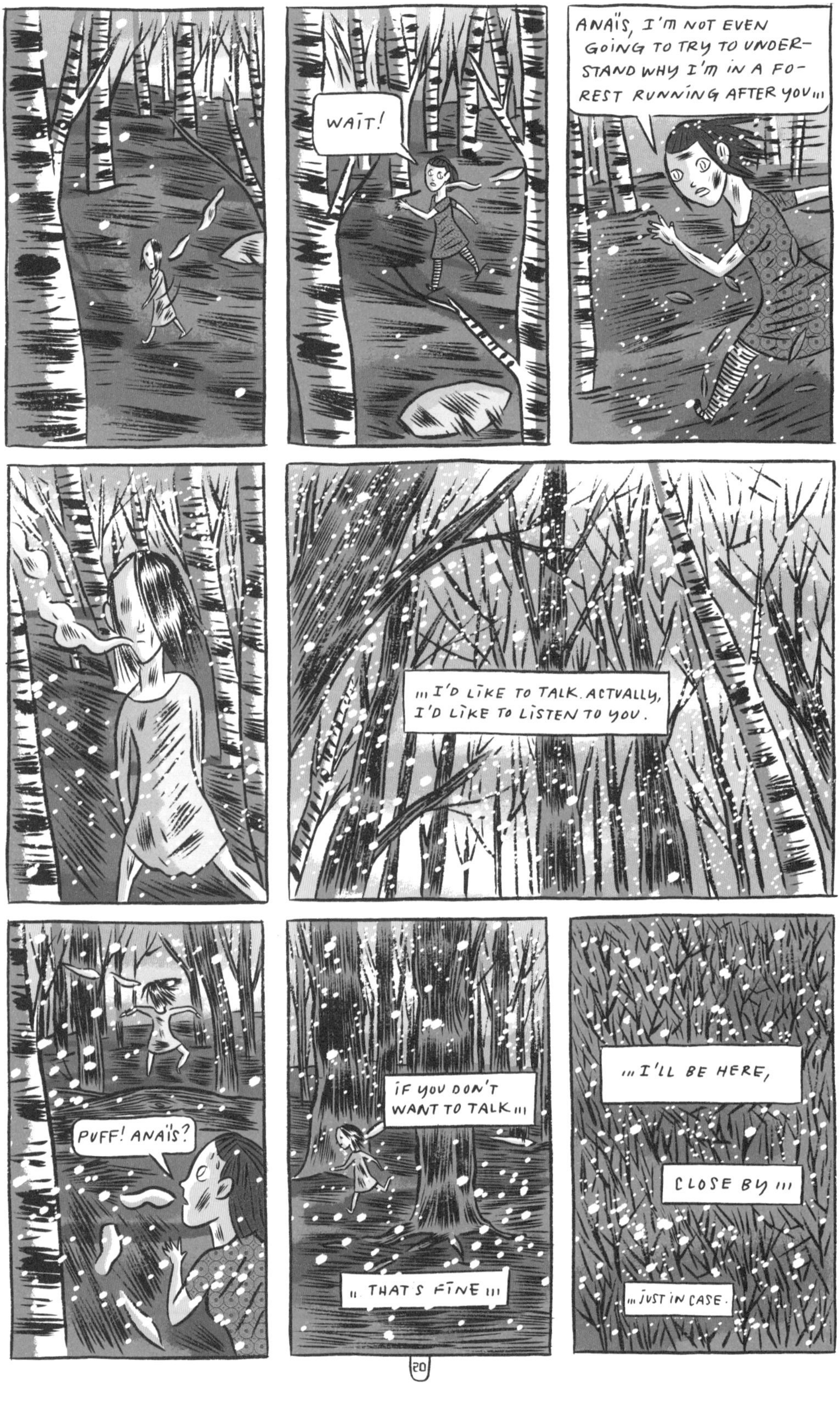
WAIT!
ANAÏS, I'M NOT EVEN GOING TO TRY TO UNDERSTAND WHY I'M IN A FOREST RUNNING AFTER YOU...
...I'D LIKE TO TALK. ACTUALLY, I'D LIKE TO LISTEN TO YOU.
PUFF! ANAÏS?
IF YOU DON'T WANT TO TALK...
.. THAT'S FINE...
...I'LL BE HERE,
CLOSE BY...
...JUST IN CASE.
20

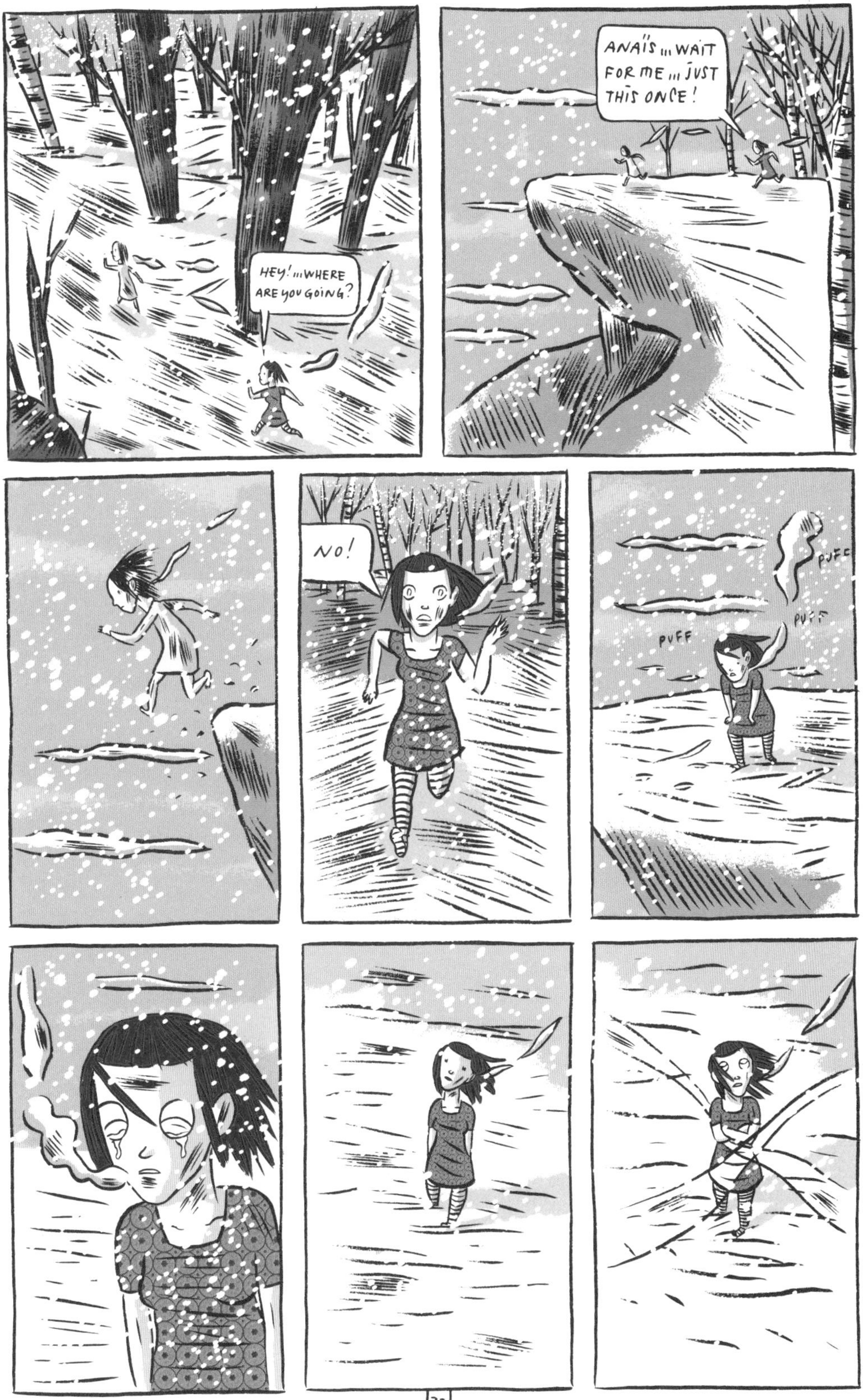
HEY! ... WHERE ARE YOU GOING?
ANAÏS ... WAIT FOR ME ... JUST THIS ONCE!
NO!
PUFF
PUFF
PUFF

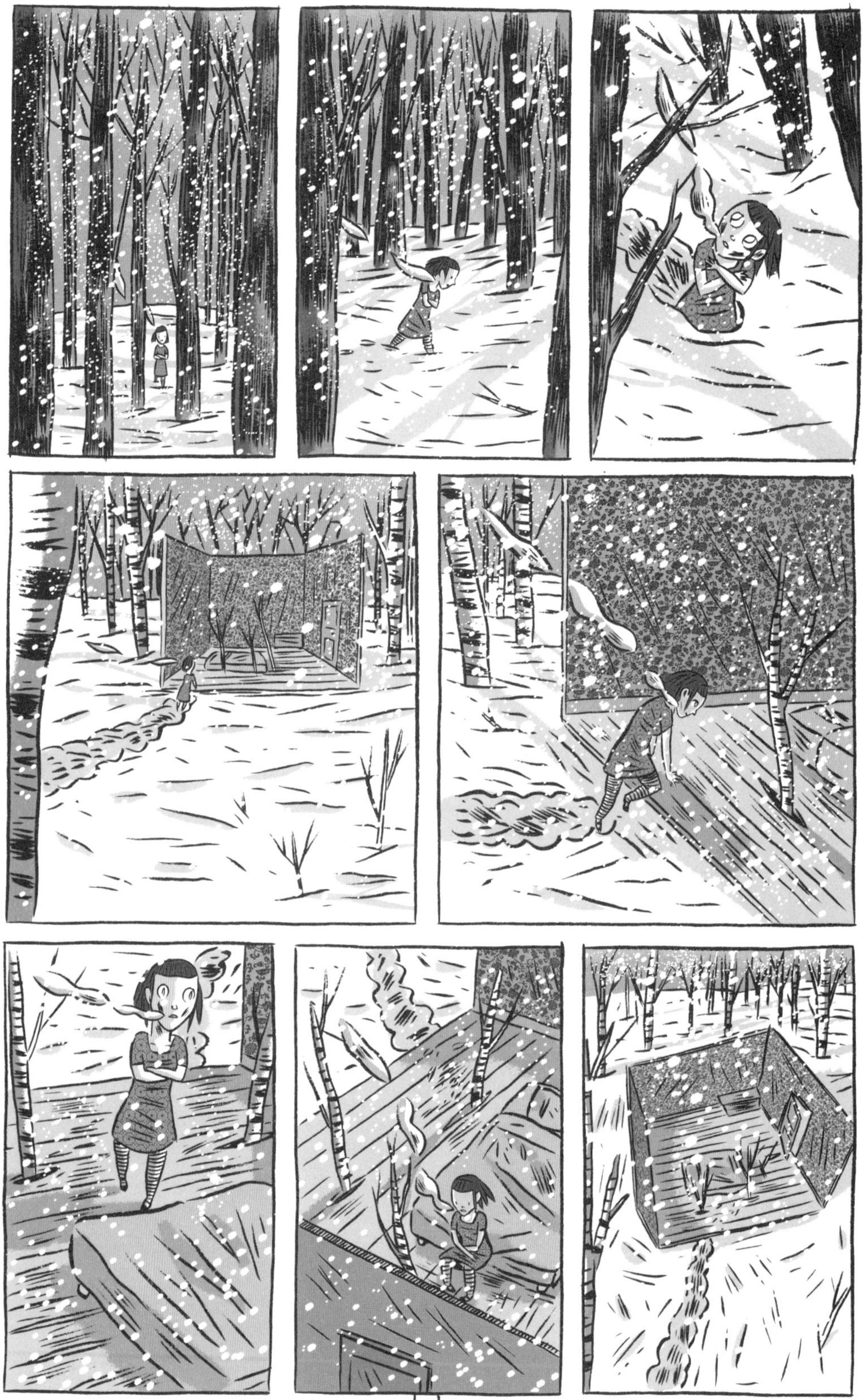

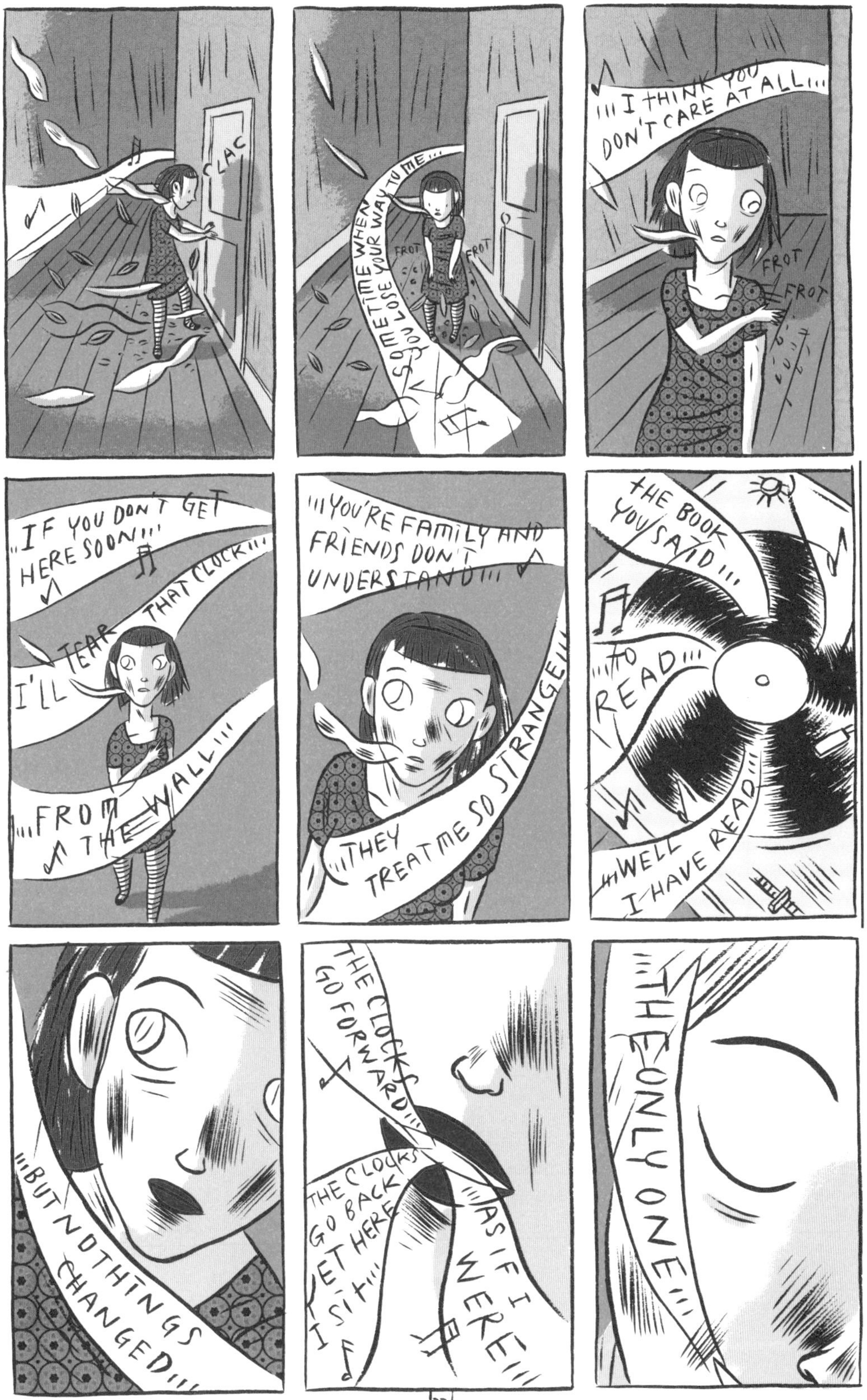
CLAC
SOMETIME WHEN YOU LOSE YOUR WAY TO ME...
FROT
FROT
...I THINK YOU DON'T CARE AT ALL...
FROT
FROT
...IF YOU DON'T GET HERE SOON...
I'LL TEAR THAT CLOCK...
...FROM THE WALL...
...YOU'RE FAMILY AND FRIENDS DON'T UNDERSTAND...
...THEY TREAT ME SO STRANGE...
THE BOOK YOU SAID...
...TO READ...
...WELL I HAVE READ...
...BUT NOTHINGS CHANGED...
THE CLOCKS GO FORWARD...
THE CLOCKS GO BACK YET HERE I SIT...
...AS IF I WERE...
...THE ONLY ONE...

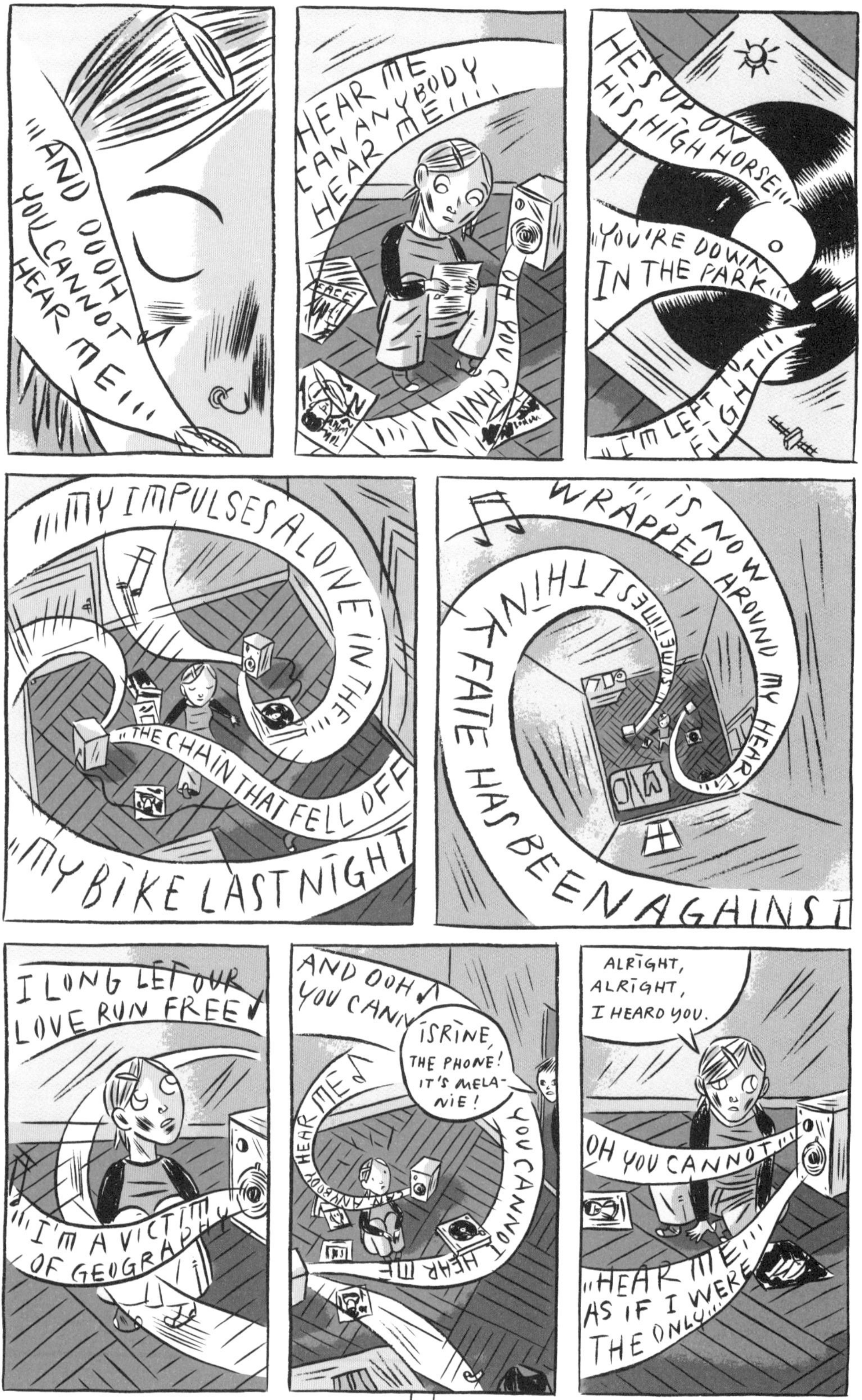
"AND OOOH YOU CANNOT HEAR ME!!!
HEAR ME CAN ANYBODY HEAR ME!!!
OH YOU CANNOT!!!
HE'S UP ON HIS HIGH HORSE!!!
YOU'RE DOWN IN THE PARK!!!
I'M LEFT TO FIGHT
MY IMPULSES ALONE IN THE
THE CHAIN THAT FELL OFF
MY BIKE LAST NIGHT
IS NOW WRAPPED AROUND MY HEART
SOMETIMES I THINK
FATE HAS BEEN AGAINST
I LONG LET OUR LOVE RUN FREE
I'M A VICTIM OF GEOGRAPHY
AND OOH YOU CANN
ISRINE, THE PHONE! IT'S MELANIE!
HEAR ME ANYBODY
YOU CANNOT HEAR ME
ALRIGHT, ALRIGHT, I HEARD YOU.
OH YOU CANNOT
HEAR ME AS IF I WERE THE ONLY

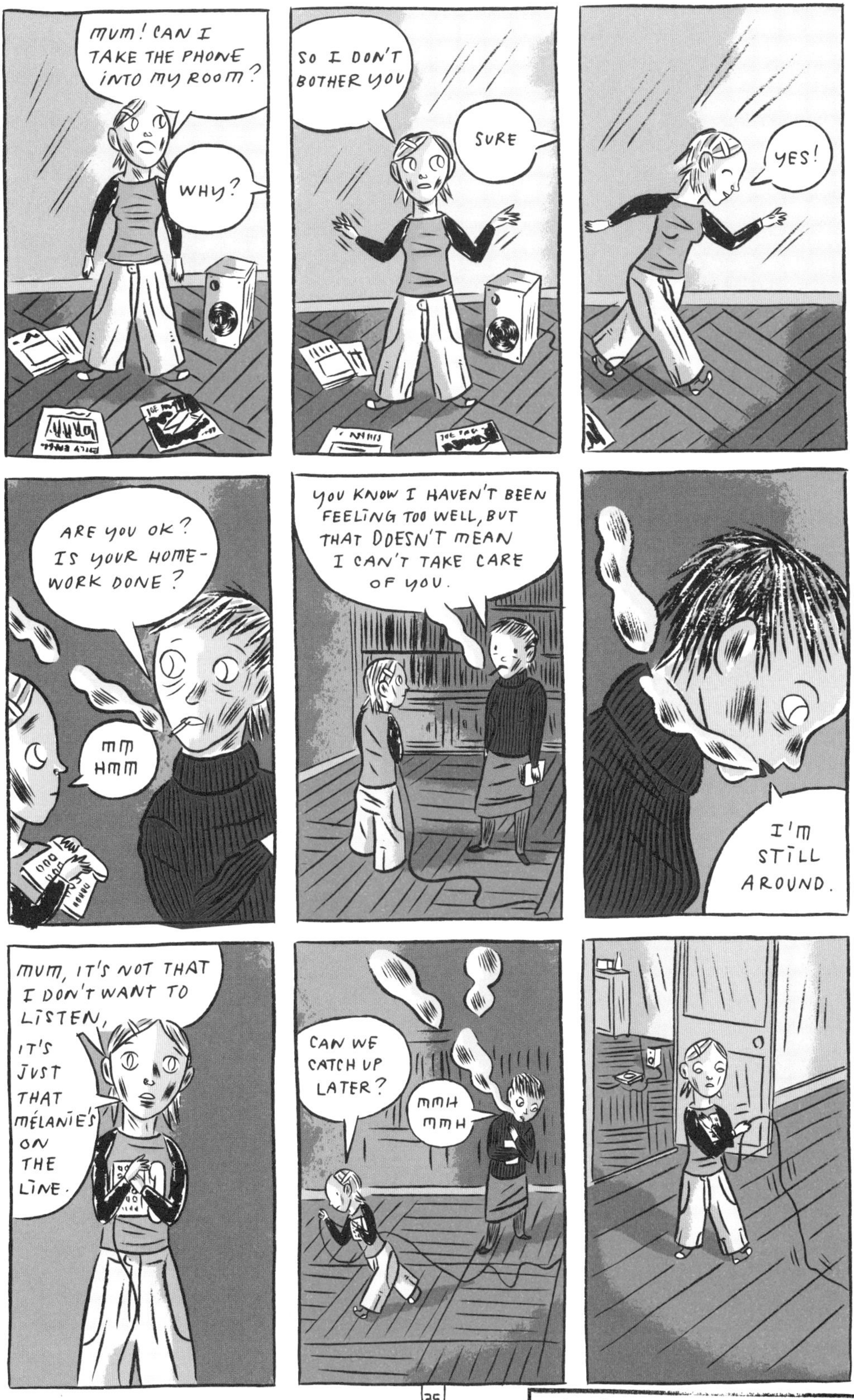
MUM! CAN I TAKE THE PHONE INTO MY ROOM?
WHY?
SO I DON'T BOTHER YOU
SURE
YES!
ARE YOU OK? IS YOUR HOME-WORK DONE?
MM HMM
YOU KNOW I HAVEN'T BEEN FEELING TOO WELL, BUT THAT DOESN'T MEAN I CAN'T TAKE CARE OF YOU.
I'M STILL AROUND.
MUM, IT'S NOT THAT I DON'T WANT TO LISTEN,
IT'S JUST THAT MÉLANIE'S ON THE LINE.
CAN WE CATCH UP LATER?
MMH MMH

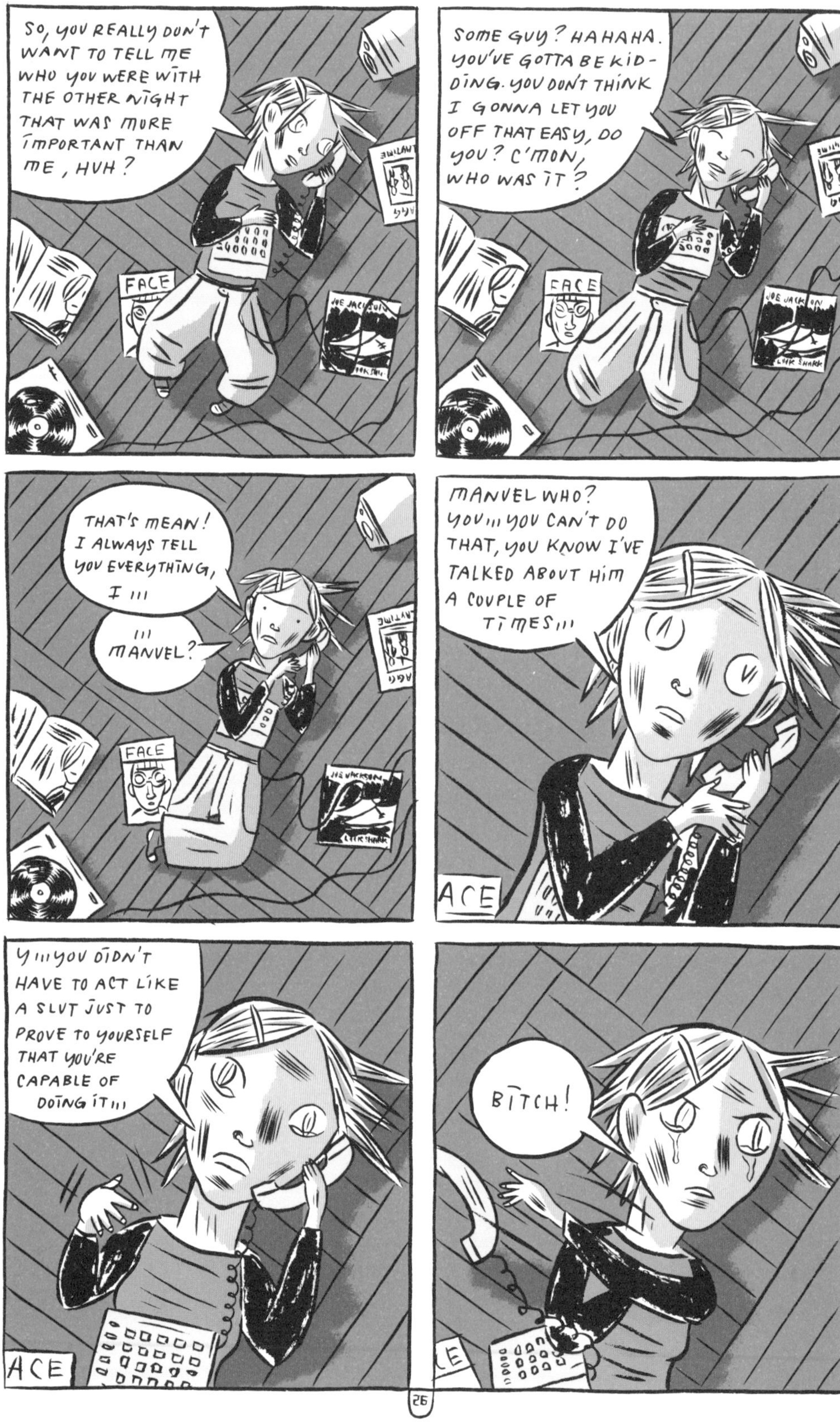
SO, YOU REALLY DON'T WANT TO TELL ME WHO YOU WERE WITH THE OTHER NIGHT THAT WAS MORE IMPORTANT THAN ME, HUH?
FACE
SOME GUY? HAHAHA. YOU'VE GOTTA BE KID-DING. YOU DON'T THINK I GONNA LET YOU OFF THAT EASY, DO YOU? C'MON, WHO WAS IT?
FACE
JOE JACKSON
THAT'S MEAN! I ALWAYS TELL YOU EVERYTHING, I ...
... MANUEL?
FACE
MANUEL WHO? YOU... YOU CAN'T DO THAT, YOU KNOW I'VE TALKED ABOUT HIM A COUPLE OF TIMES...
ACE
Y... YOU DIDN'T HAVE TO ACT LIKE A SLUT JUST TO PROVE TO YOURSELF THAT YOU'RE CAPABLE OF DOING IT...
ACE
BITCH!

TUUUT
THAT SUCKS!
CLAC
PFFFFF
FACE
JOE JACKSON
RING RING
GO TO HELL! GO TO HELL!
LEAVE ME ALONE!
RINGING
RING

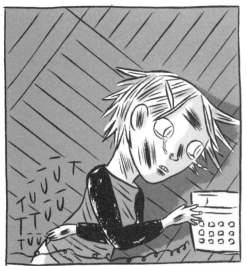

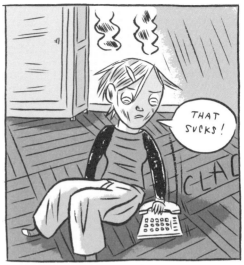

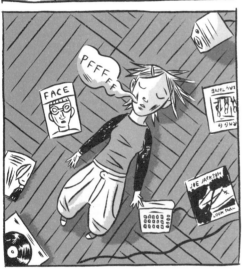

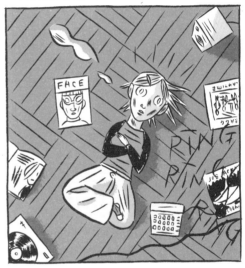

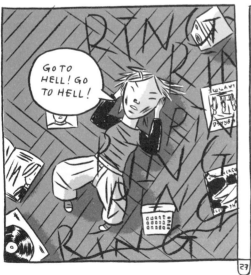

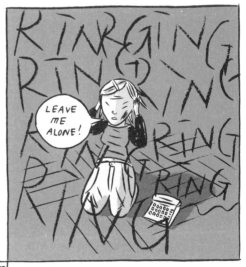

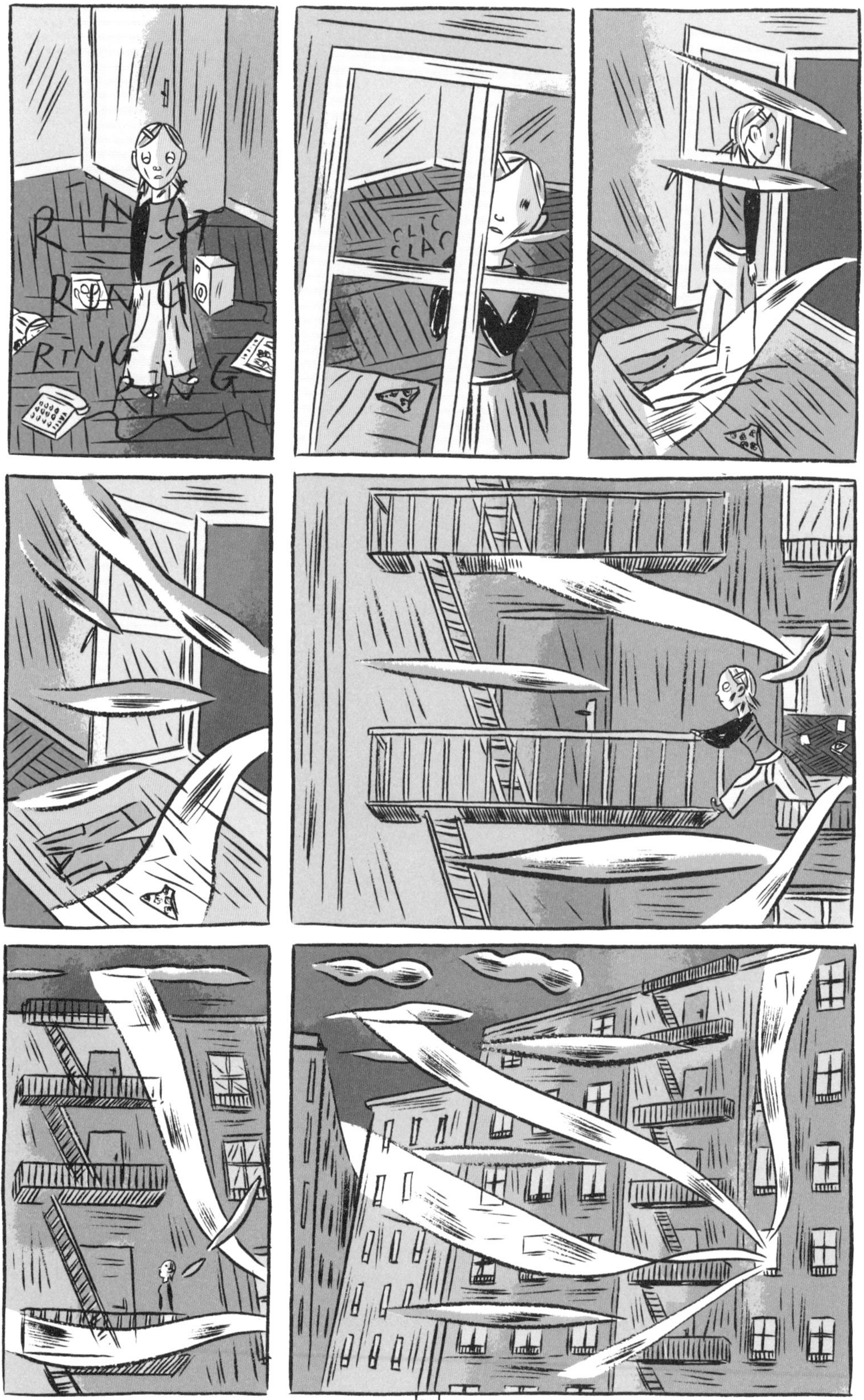
RING
RING
RING
RING
CLIC
CLAC

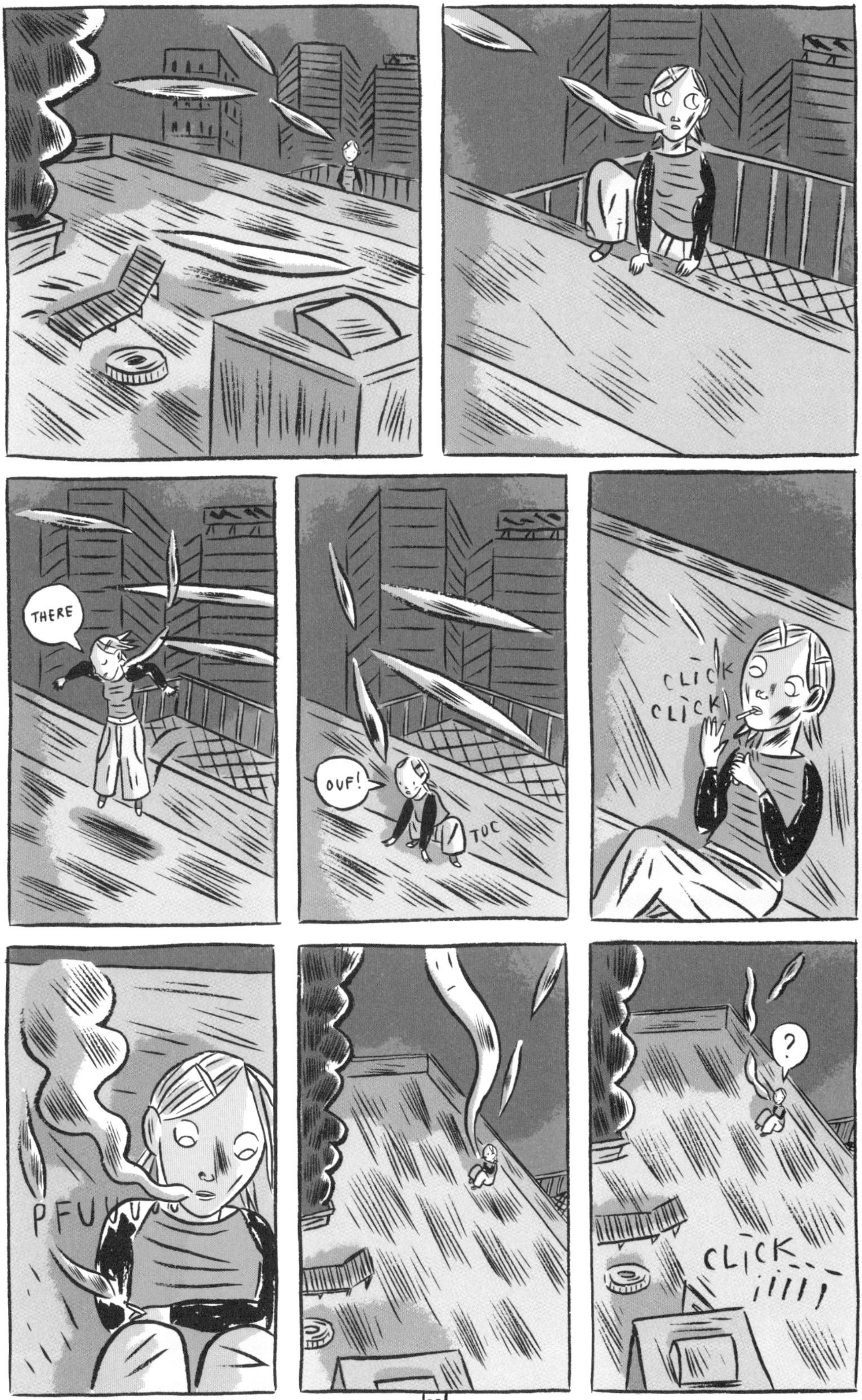
THERE
OUF!
TUC
CLICK
CLICK
PFUUUU
?
CLICK

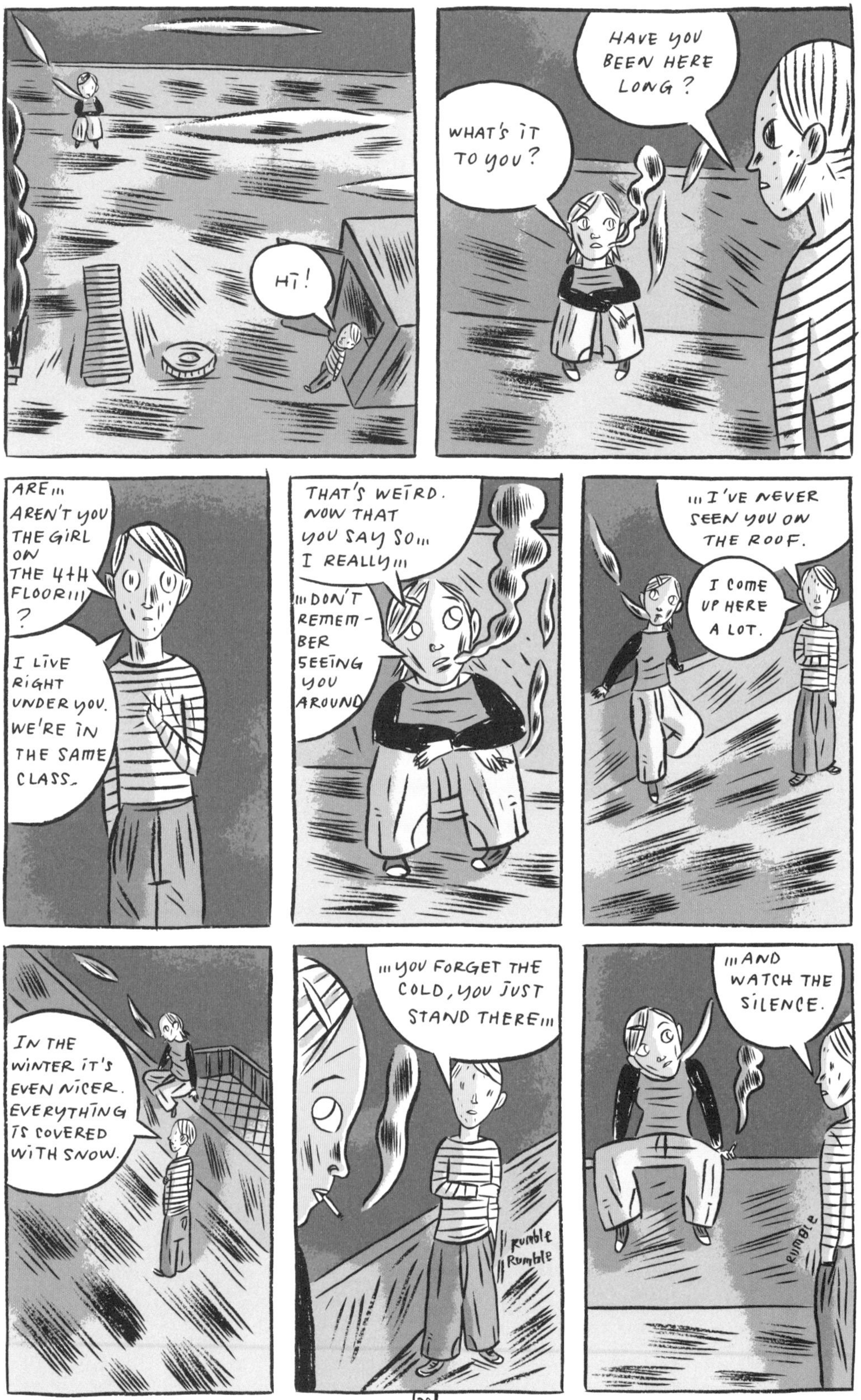
HI!
HAVE YOU BEEN HERE LONG?
WHAT'S IT TO YOU?
ARE... AREN'T YOU THE GIRL ON THE 4TH FLOOR... ?
I LIVE RIGHT UNDER YOU. WE'RE IN THE SAME CLASS.
THAT'S WEIRD. NOW THAT YOU SAY SO... I REALLY...
...DON'T REMEMBER SEEING YOU AROUND
...I'VE NEVER SEEN YOU ON THE ROOF.
I COME UP HERE A LOT.
IN THE WINTER IT'S EVEN NICER. EVERYTHING IS COVERED WITH SNOW.
...YOU FORGET THE COLD, YOU JUST STAND THERE...
rumble rumble
...AND WATCH THE SILENCE.
RUMBLE

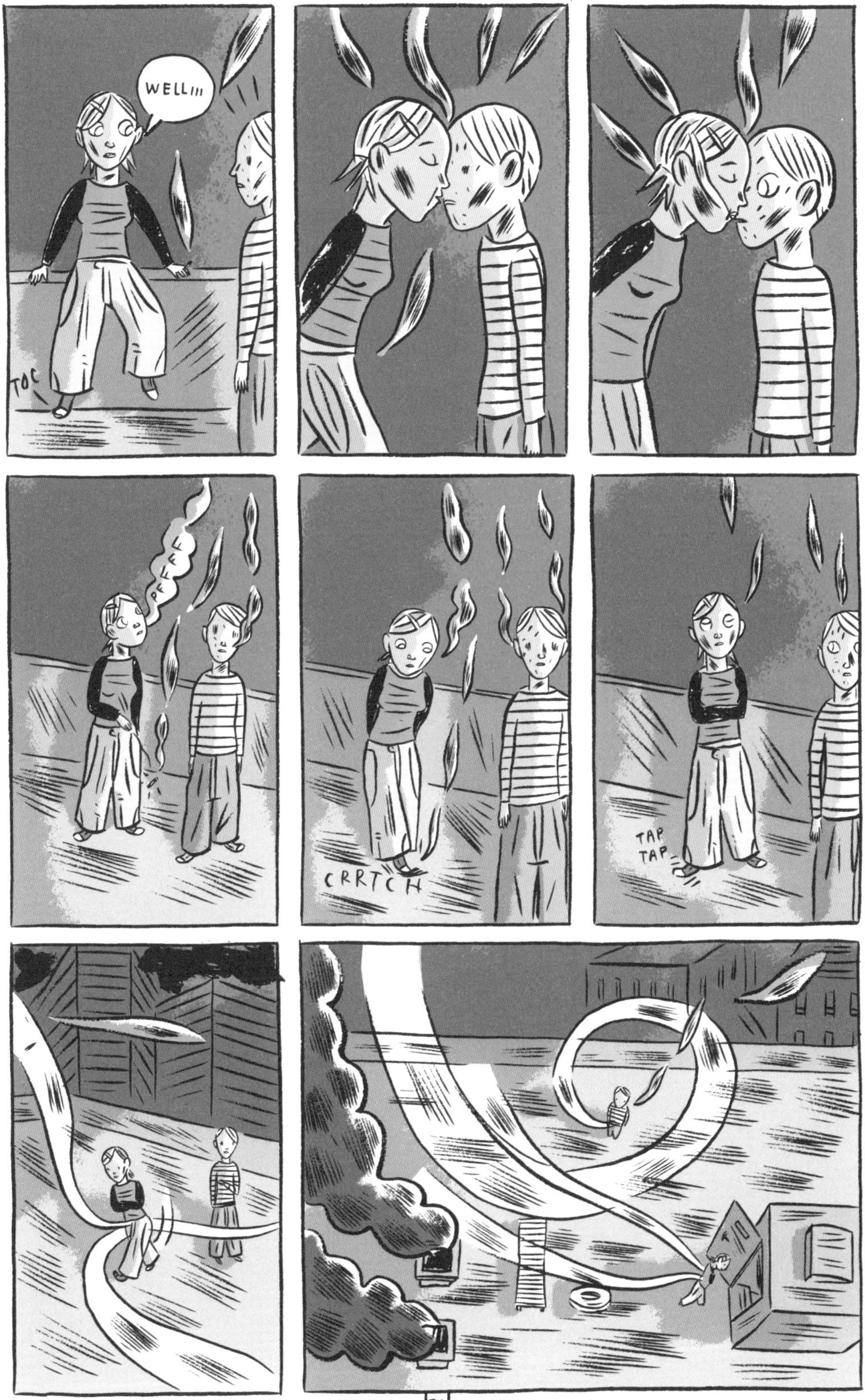
WELL!!!
TOC
PFFFF
CRRTCH
TAP TAP

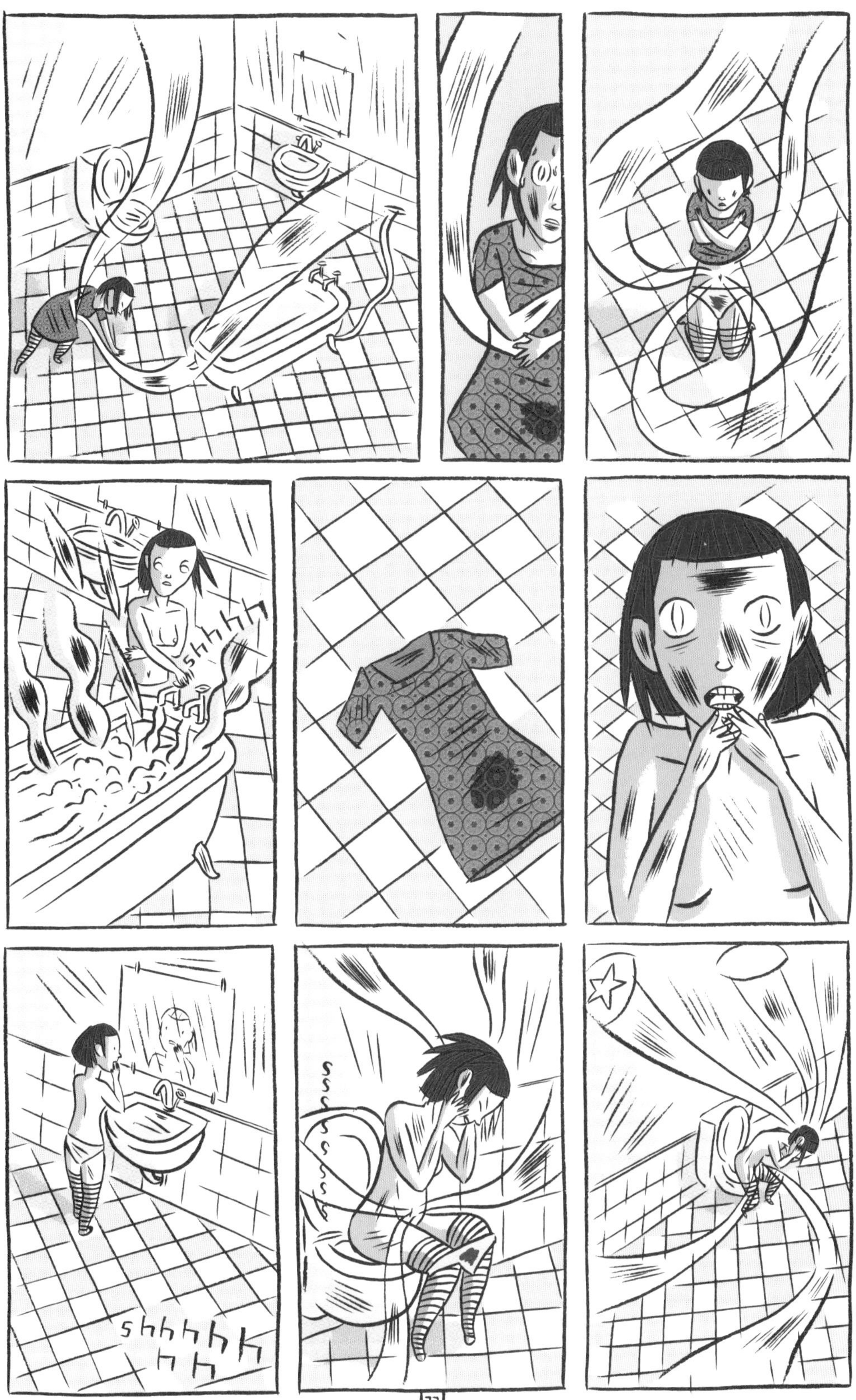
shhhhh
shhhhh
hh
ssssssss

SSSHH
?
POC
HA!
QUACK!
I REALLY DON'T UNDERSTAND...
...WHY YOU'RE SO UPSET.
I'M NOT UPSET ...YOU'RE UPSETTING ME...
YOU SAID WE COULD TALK THINGS OVER.
I CHANGED MY MIND.
YOU'RE MAKING THIS EANY EASIER FOR ISRINE. IT'S...
...HARD ENOUGH AS IT IS TO EXPLAIN TO HER WHAT'S GOING ON BETWEEN US...

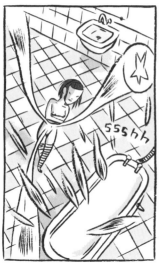

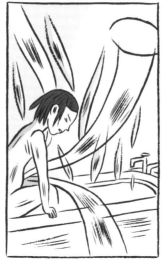

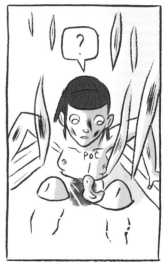

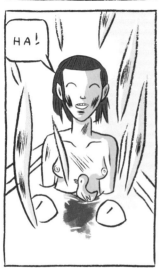

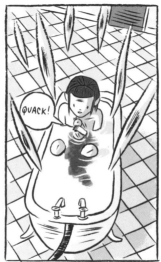

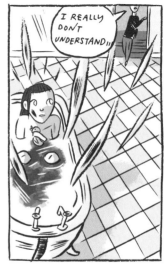

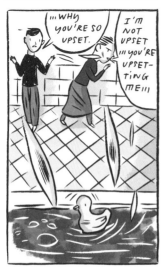

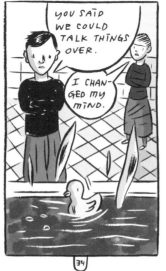

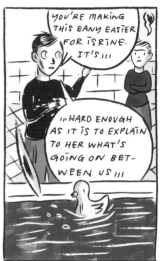

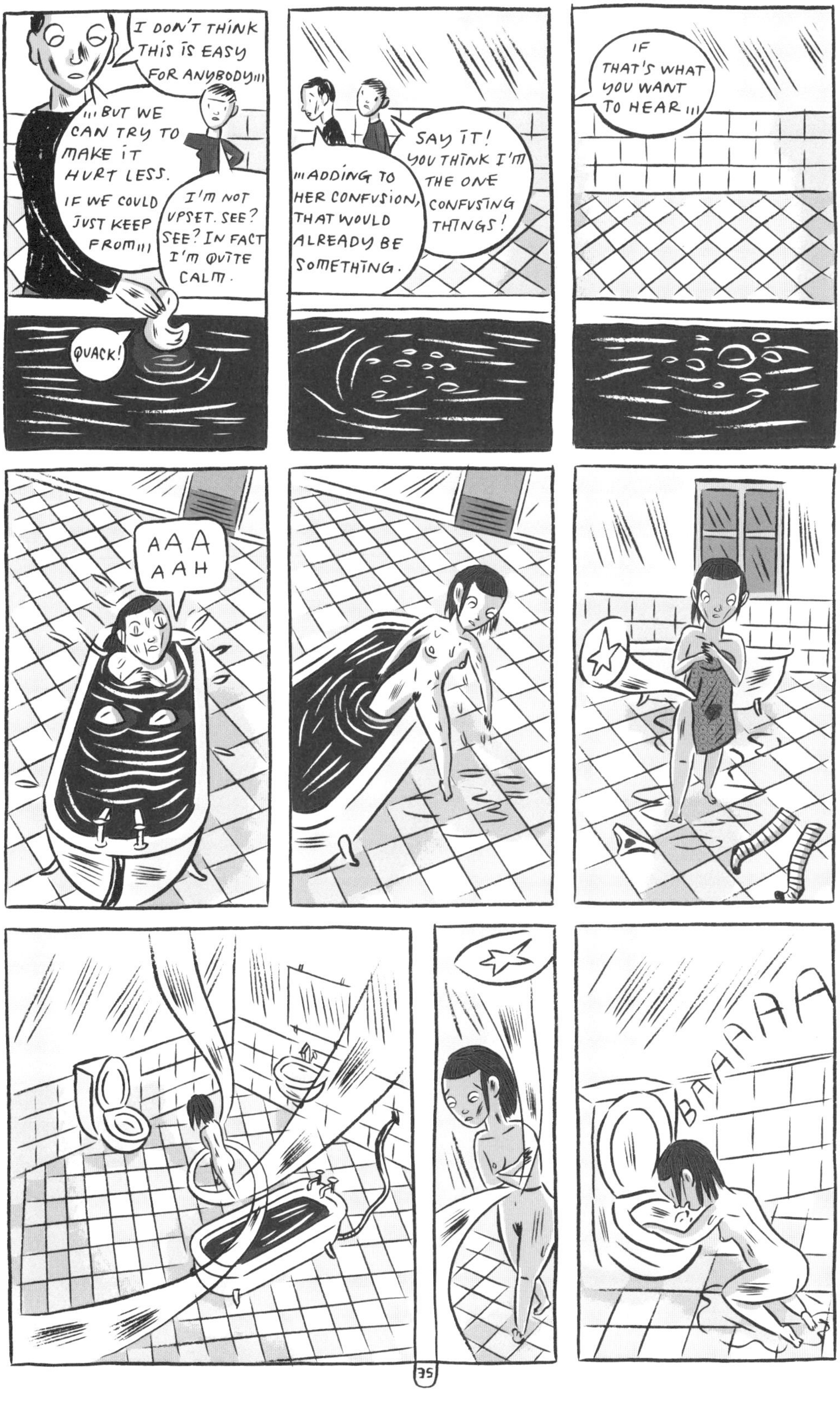
I DON'T THINK THIS IS EASY FOR ANYBODY...
...BUT WE CAN TRY TO MAKE IT HURT LESS. IF WE COULD JUST KEEP FROM...
I'M NOT UPSET. SEE? SEE? IN FACT I'M QUITE CALM.
QUACK!
...ADDING TO HER CONFUSION, THAT WOULD ALREADY BE SOMETHING.
SAY IT! YOU THINK I'M THE ONE CONFUSING THINGS!
IF THAT'S WHAT YOU WANT TO HEAR...
AAA AAH
BAAAAA
35

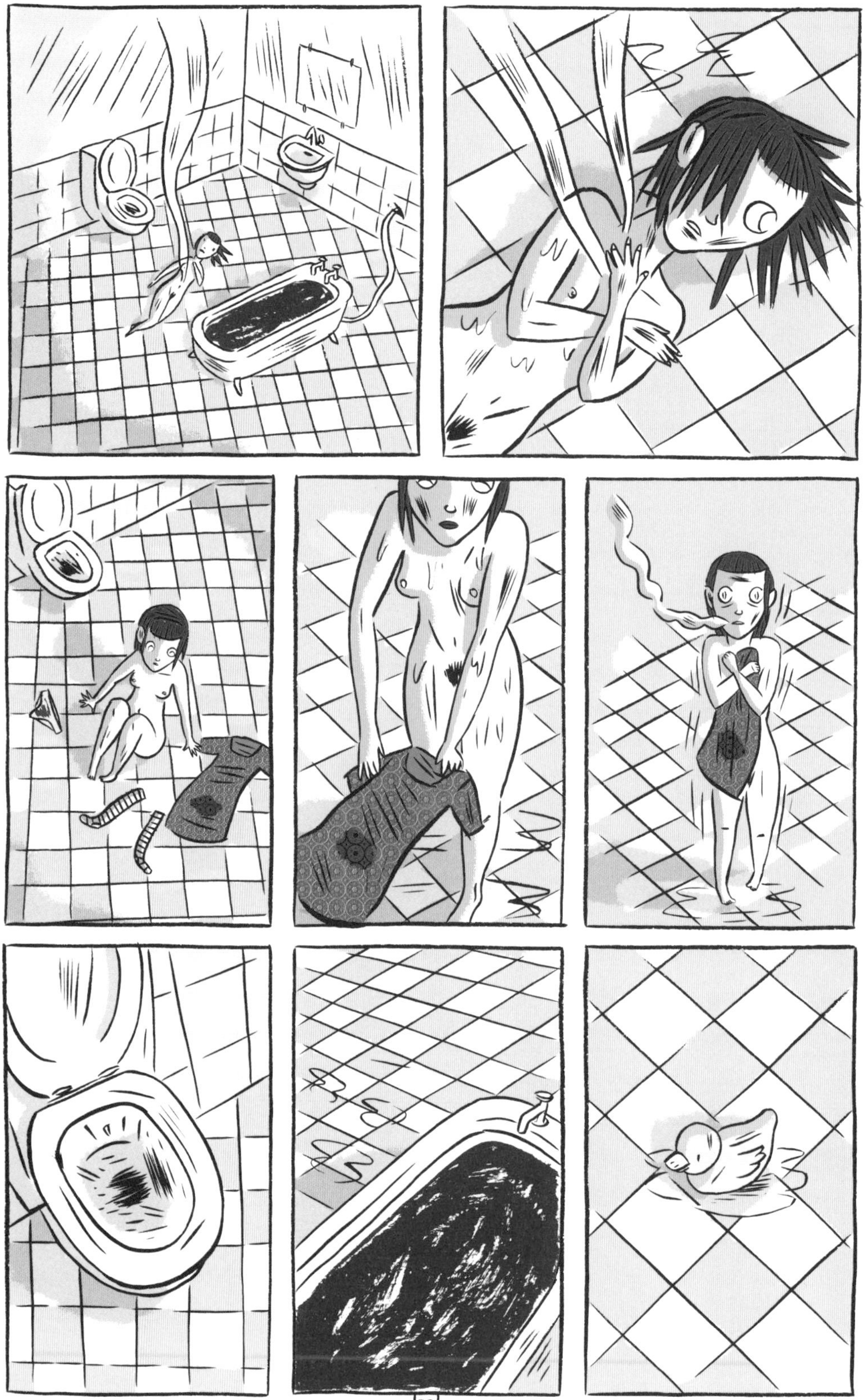
36

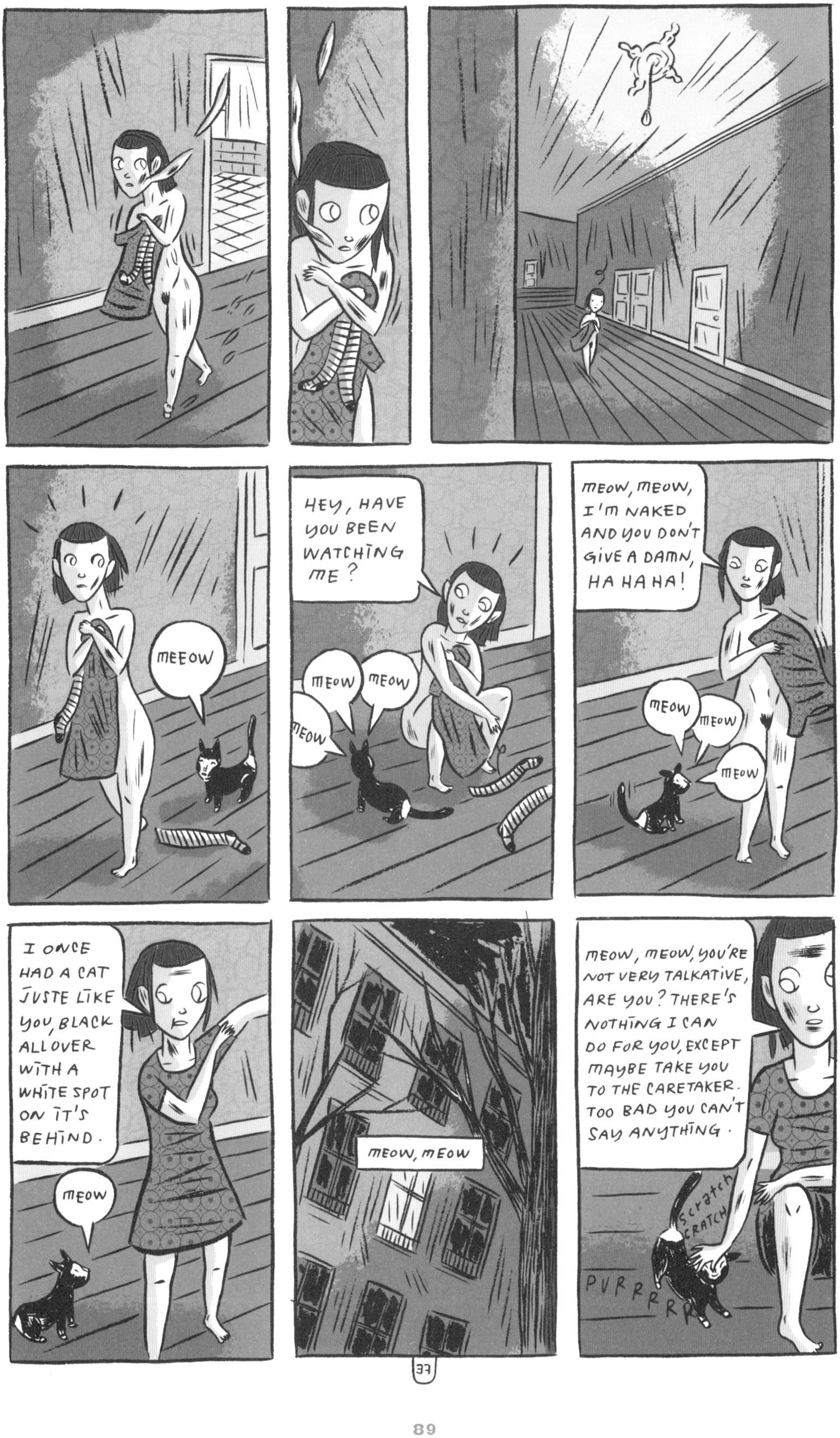

MEEOW
HEY, HAVE YOU BEEN WATCHING ME?
MEOW
MEOW
MEOW
MEOW, MEOW, I'M NAKED AND YOU DON'T GIVE A DAMN, HA HA HA!
MEOW
MEOW
MEOW
I ONCE HAD A CAT JUSTE LIKE YOU, BLACK ALL OVER WITH A WHITE SPOT ON IT'S BEHIND.
MEOW
MEOW, MEOW
MEOW, MEOW, YOU'RE NOT VERY TALKATIVE, ARE YOU? THERE'S NOTHING I CAN DO FOR YOU, EXCEPT MAYBE TAKE YOU TO THE CARETAKER. TOO BAD YOU CAN'T SAY ANYTHING.
SCRATCH SCRATCH
PURRRRRR
37

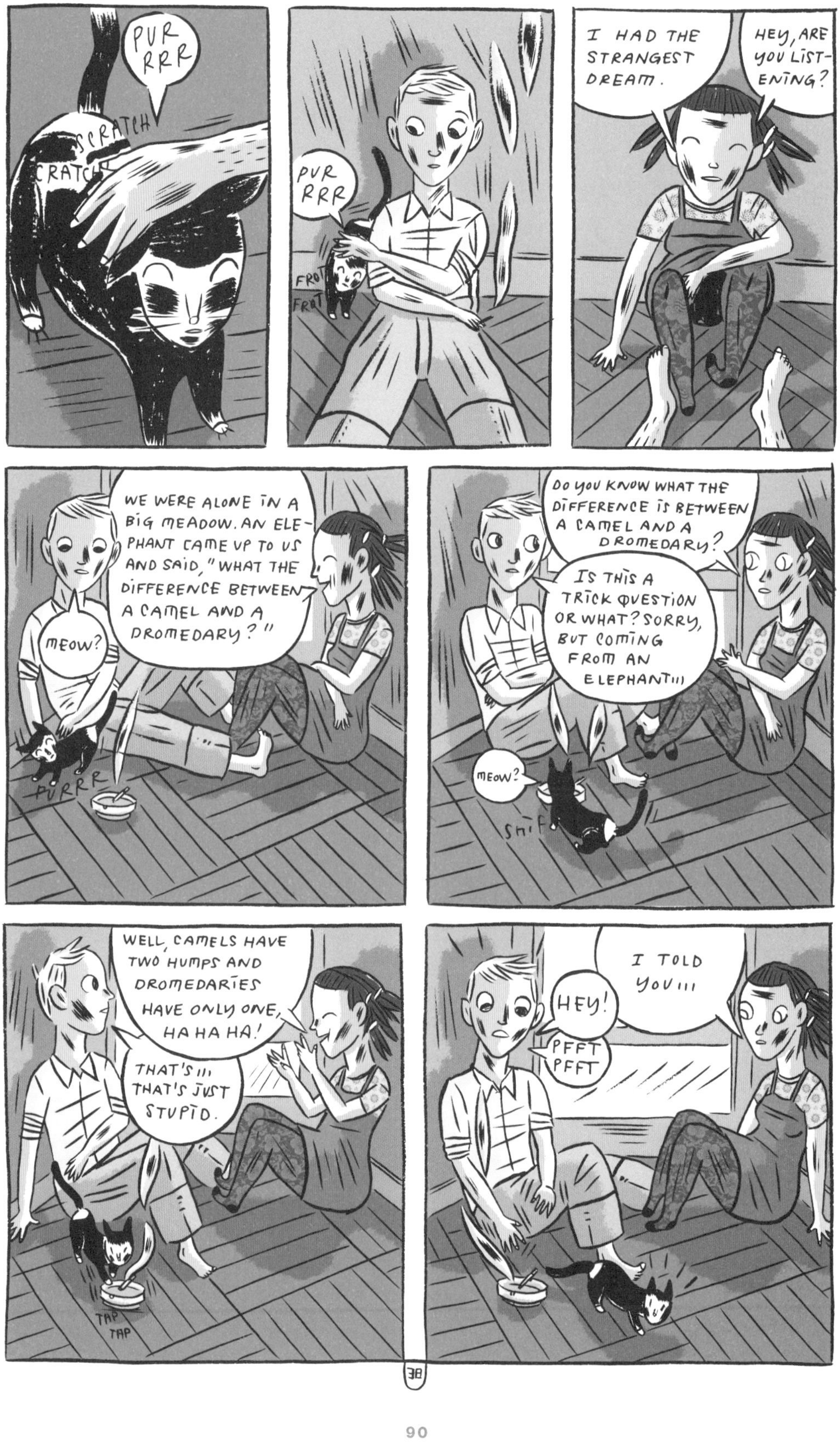
PUR RRR
SCRATCH
SCRATCH
PUR RRR
FROT
FROT
I HAD THE STRANGEST DREAM.
HEY, ARE YOU LISTENING?
WE WERE ALONE IN A BIG MEADOW. AN ELEPHANT CAME UP TO US AND SAID, "WHAT THE DIFFERENCE BETWEEN A CAMEL AND A DROMEDARY?"
MEOW?
PURRR
DO YOU KNOW WHAT THE DIFFERENCE IS BETWEEN A CAMEL AND A DROMEDARY?
IS THIS A TRICK QUESTION OR WHAT? SORRY, BUT COMING FROM AN ELEPHANT...
MEOW?
SNIF
WELL, CAMELS HAVE TWO HUMPS AND DROMEDARIES HAVE ONLY ONE, HA HA HA!
THAT'S... THAT'S JUST STUPID.
TAP
TAP
I TOLD YOU...
HEY!
PFFT PFFT
38

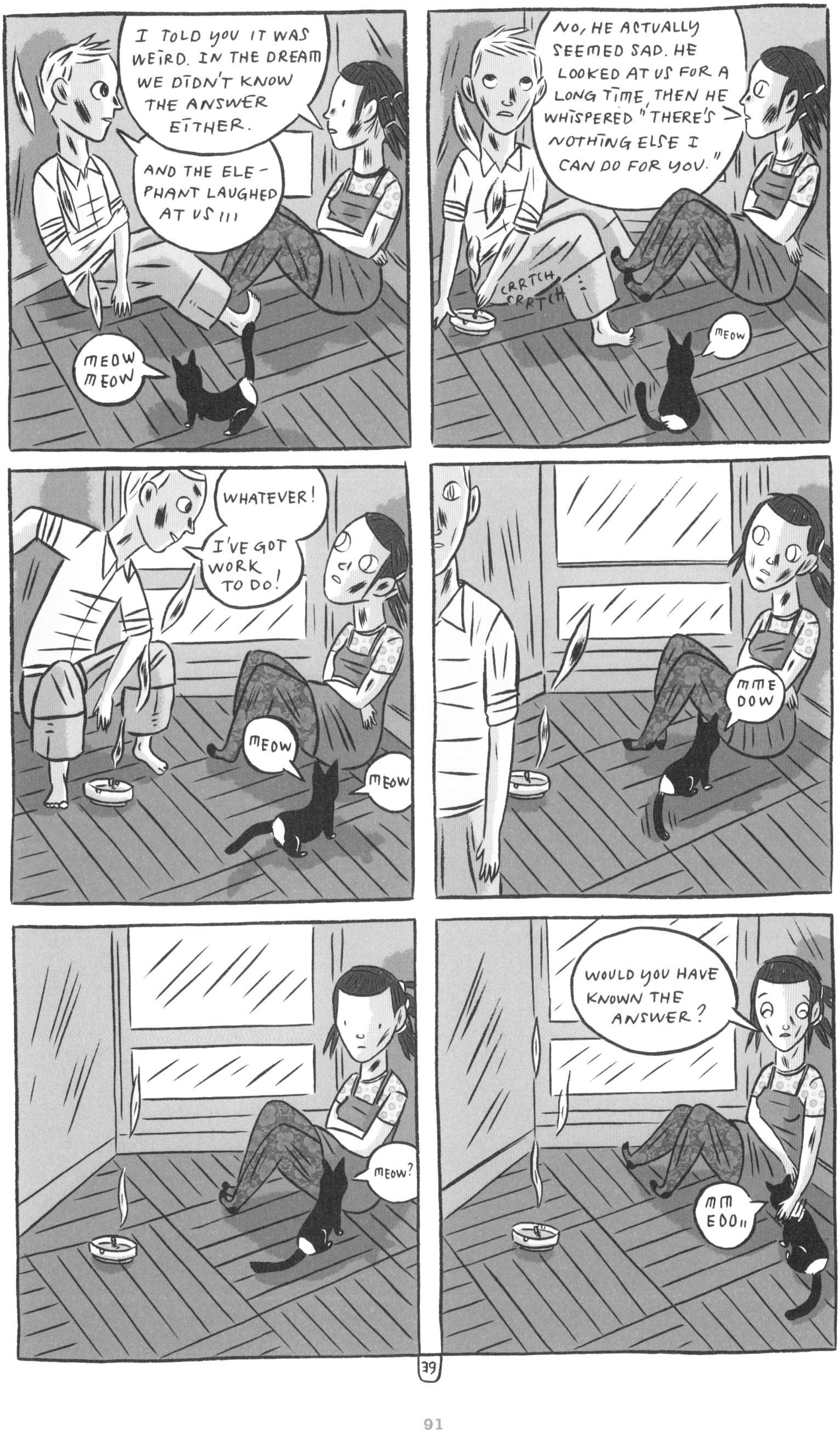
I TOLD YOU IT WAS WEIRD. IN THE DREAM WE DIDN'T KNOW THE ANSWER EITHER.
AND THE ELE-PHANT LAUGHED AT US!!!
MEOW MEOW
NO, HE ACTUALLY SEEMED SAD. HE LOOKED AT US FOR A LONG TIME, THEN HE WHISPERED "THERE'S NOTHING ELSE I CAN DO FOR YOU."
CRRTCH CRRTCH
MEOW
WHATEVER!
I'VE GOT WORK TO DO!
MEOW
MEOW
MME DOW
MEOW?
WOULD YOU HAVE KNOWN THE ANSWER?
MM EDO!!
39

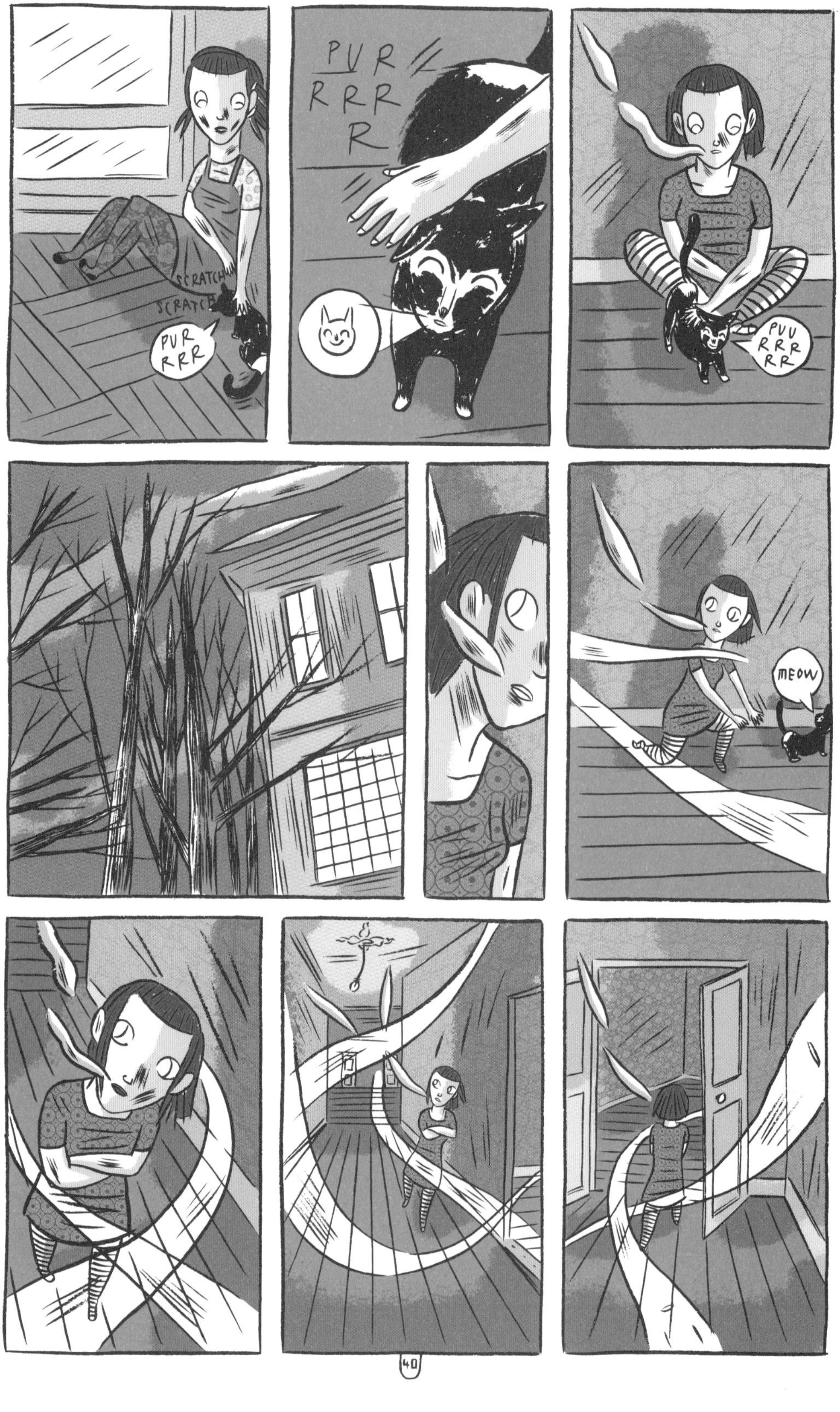
SCRATCH
SCRATCH
PUR RRR
PUR RRR R
PUU RRR RR
MEOW

40

47

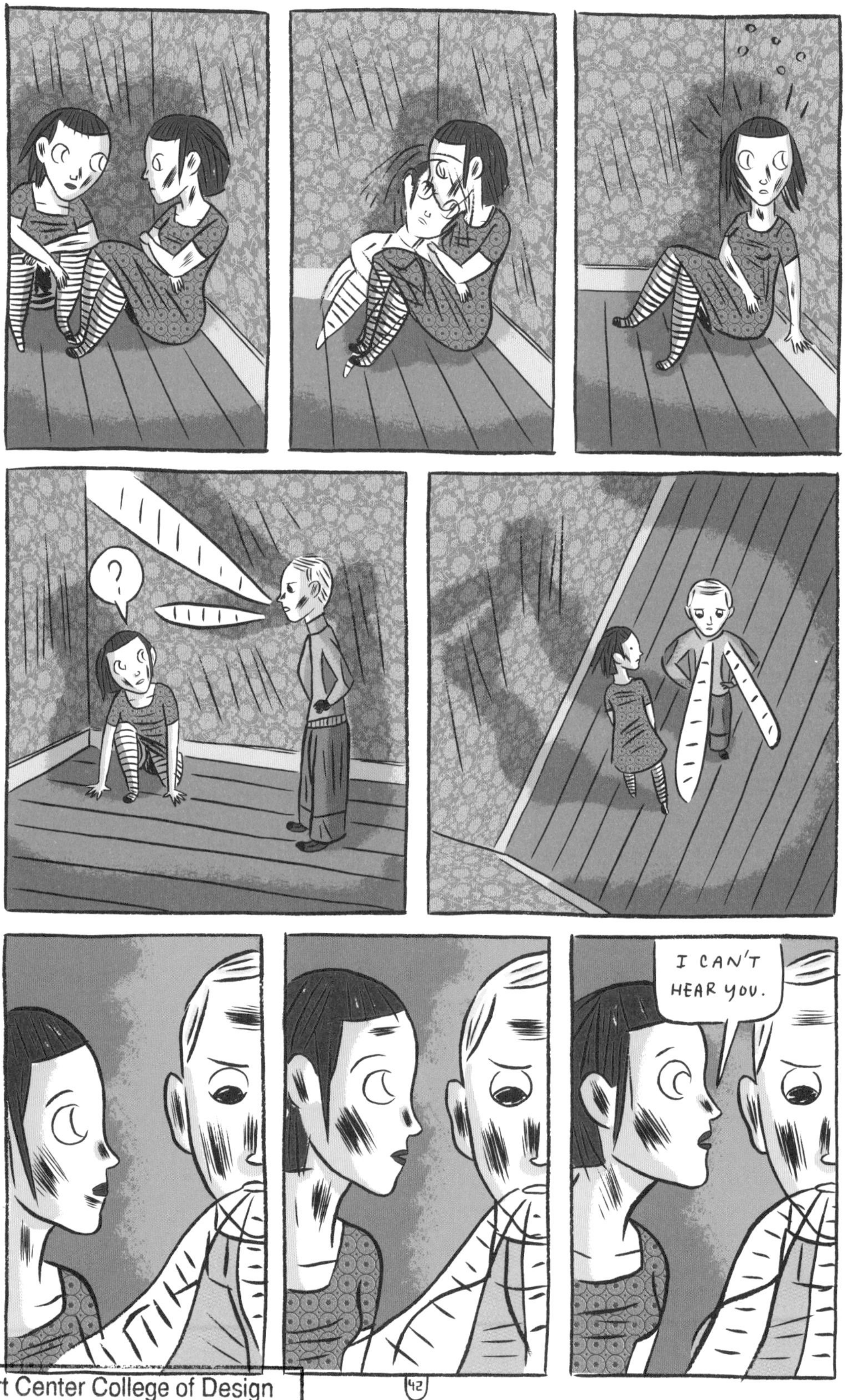
?
I CAN'T HEAR YOU.

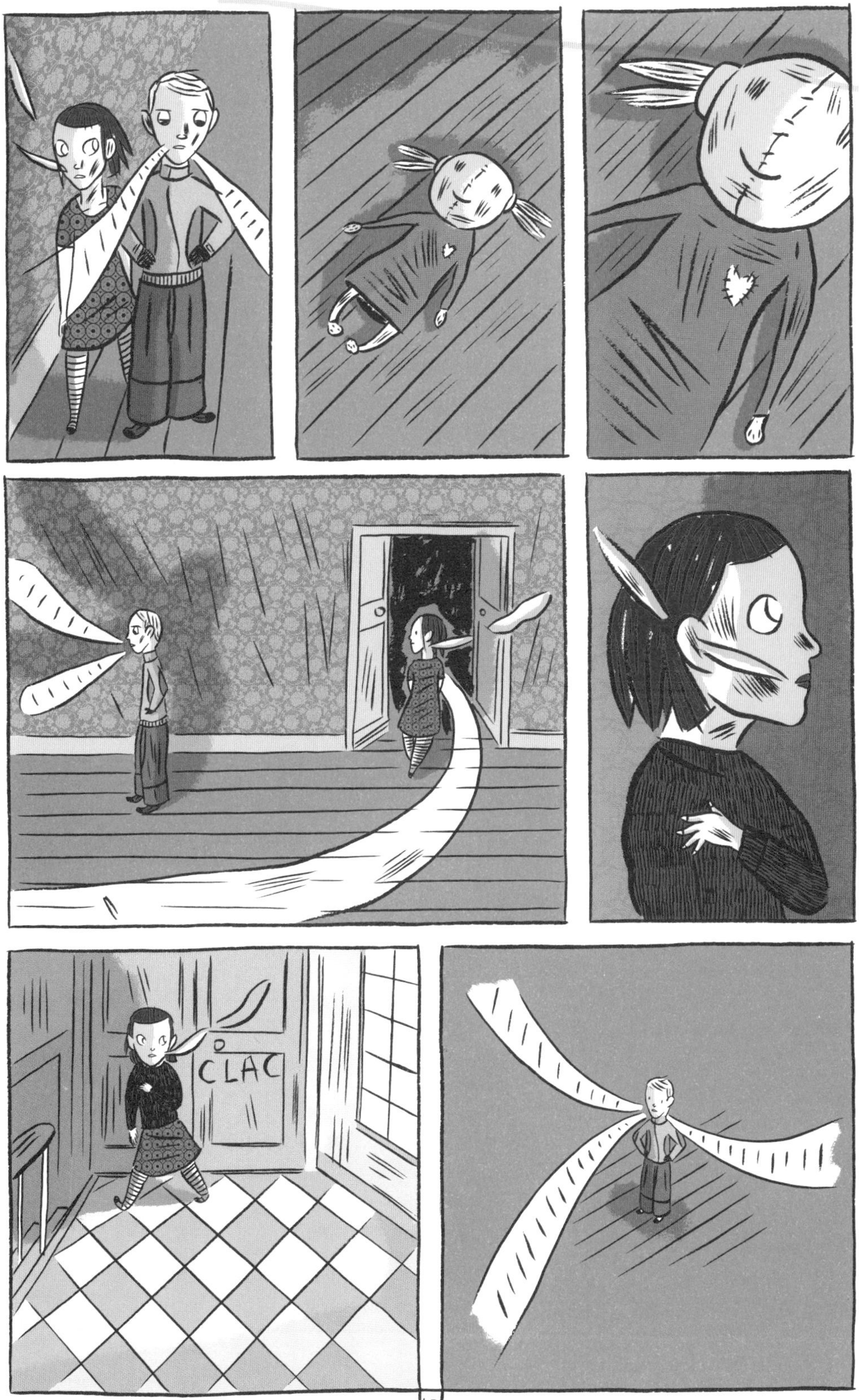
CLAC
43

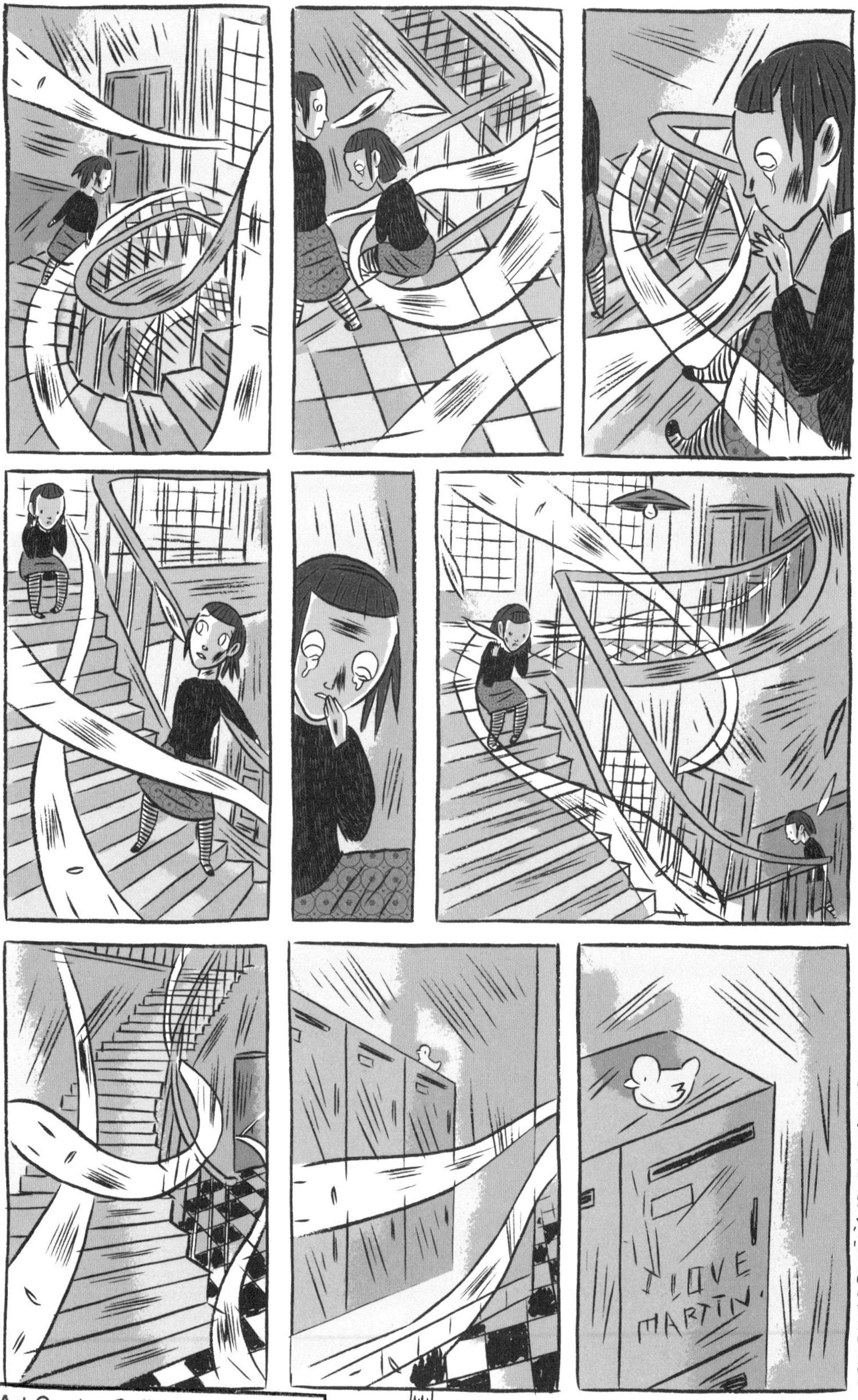
I LOVE MARTIN.
44

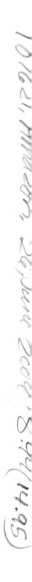

MANY THANKS TO HEIDI & AEL FOR THEIR PATIENCE. LOVE.

NICOLAS, 03